Portrait of
PASTA

Portrait of
PASTA

Anna Del Conte

**PADDINGTON
PRESS LTD**

**THE TWO CONTINENTS
PUBLISHING GROUP**

Library of Congress Cataloging in Publication Data

Del Conte, Anna.
   Portrait of Pasta.

   Includes indexes.
   1. Cookery (Macaroni) 2. Macaroni products.
I. Title.
TX809.M17D44   641.8'22   75-22952
ISBN 0-8467-0106-5

Computer typeset by Input Typesetting Ltd.
4 Valentine Place, London S.E.1. England

Cover design by Richard Browner
Cover illustration by David Bull
Drawings by Charlotte Knox
Designed by Richard Johnson & Colin Lewis
Picture research by Nora Stein

IN THE UNITED STATES
PADDINGTON PRESS LTD
TWO CONTINENTS PUBLISHING GROUP
30 East 42 Street, New York City, N.Y. 10017

IN THE UNITED KINGDOM
PADDINGTON PRESS LTD
231 The Vale London W3

IN CANADA distributed by
RANDOM HOUSE OF CANADA LTD
5390 Ambler Drive
Mississauga, Ontario L4W 1Y7

Table of Contents

I should like to thank the following people for the help and encouragement given me in the writing of this book.

Mr. Robert M. Green, The National Macaroni Institute, Palatine, Illinois, U.S.A.
Dr. Lella Mariani, Casa Editrice Rizzoli, Milan, Italy
Dr. Martino Pizzetti, Pastificio Braibanti, Parma, Italy
Dr. Corrado Sirolli, Fara S. Martino, Italy
Mr. K. L. Spencer, Pasta Foods Ltd., St. Albans, England
Dr. Livio Zupicich, I.B.P. Industrie Buitoni Perugina, Perugia, Italy

My particular thanks and appreciation are due to Ing. Vincenzo Agnesi for having given me so much of his time, and for the rich harvest of information I was able to gather from his Museum in Pontedassio and his writings.

Introduction

The scene is a little restaurant – dimly lit – candles on the tables giving a cosy glow. In the corner sits a young couple, hand in hand across the gingham cloth, gazing into each other's eyes. As we join them their hands part, for a friendly old waiter has padded up to their table. Now, smiling his approval, he sets before each of them a plate that is piled high, steaming, glistening. "Your spaghetti" he says.

It had to be spaghetti. For pasta is the food – if not of love – certainly of close companionship. A glance at the many generations of an Italian family sitting around a large table, noisily partaking of the spaghetti ritual, says all there is to say about the importance of pasta as a shared experience.

Pasta knows no barriers of class or wealth. In Italy it is a favorite with princes and peasants alike (in Italy such anachronisms still exist), and elsewhere in the world pasta may be part of a banquet or it may be just a simple supper. Pasta knows no national barriers either. Although a national dish – what other food is so strongly identified with one country? – it is eaten all over the world. Pasta is the simplest food there is – just wheat and water – and yet it can assume a hundred different tastes, from cream to curry, from spinach to sardines. Pasta is also the most versatile food there is, for it can be a first course, main dish, side dish or even dessert.

So read on. Find out about Yankee Doodle's macaroni, study closely the picture of the spaghetti tree, discover why pasta is not fattening. And when you have read your fill, choose a sauce that suits your mood, boil up that saucepan of water; then, with due reverence, open up the package of pasta – or reach proudly for the pasta you have made yourself. The moment of truth is at hand.

7

What pasta is

What is pasta made of? What goes into that long list of ingredients? Flour and water, that's all. Except that this kind of flour is called semolina. And what is semolina? Read on.

Triticum Durum

In the beginning there was the genus *Triticum* of the family *Graminae.* In other words: wheat. Wheat has been the basic foodstuff of man, it seems, since the year dot. Nor have things changed all that much, since even today half the world's population would starve without wheat. Rice feeds the other half.

There are hundreds of different varieties of wheat, but the two of outstanding importance are *Triticum vulgare,* or common wheat, from which bread is made, and *Triticum durum,* or durum wheat, sometimes known as macaroni wheat. It is called durum, the Latin for hard, because its grains are far harder than those of common wheat. Grinding the grains of common wheat produces the familiar powdery flour used for making bread and in cooking generally. When the grains of durum wheat are ground they produce a substance which has the consistency of sugar, and is made up of sharp, hard amber-colored granules. This is semolina, and it is from this, and water, that pasta is made.

A Place Called Taganrog

Durum wheat has grown in countries bordering the Mediterranean since antiquity. In the nineteenth century, however, Russia was one of the main producers of durum wheat, and Russian durum was known as the very best. There was a big export trade in durum wheat to Italy for pasta making, and this centered around the port of Taganrog. Taganrog is on the Sea of Azov, which is a small sea joined by a strait to the northeast corner of the Black Sea. The grain that was shipped from there to Venice, Genoa and Naples in the nineteenth century grew abundantly in the Ukraine, in the rich fertile valleys of the Don and the lower Volga. So fertile is the black earth there that there is a proverb in that part of Russia: "Sow stones, and wheat will grow."

The fine durum wheat that was shipped to Italy was known as Taganrog wheat, and the best pasta makers of the day would use no other. Indeed, late in

Golden grains of durum wheat from Canada being unloaded at Great Yarmouth, England, ready for milling into semolina.

the nineteenth century, before local manufacture had really taken over in America, when half the entire output of one Neapolitan pasta manufacturer was consumed in New York State, the packages were proudly marked "*Pasta di Taganrog.*"

This once well-known port can claim a fascinating footnote in the pages of Italian history. At Taganrog in 1833 an Italian sailor called Giovanni Cuneo, only twenty-four at the time, was holding forth in a bar crowded with Italian seamen about the shameful plight of Italy — a country then divided and largely under foreign rule. Cuneo himself was under threat of arrest as a follower of Mazzini and a member of *Giovane Italia* (Young Italy). At the back of the room stood a young blond sailor listening with suppressed excitement. After a while, fired by the vision of a united Italy and unable to contain his emotion any longer, he ran up to Cuneo and embraced him. The blond youth was Garibaldi, the moment was the birth of his lifelong crusade to unify Italy, and the place was Taganrog. On June 3, 1961, Kruschev unveiled a stone that commemorates the event.

However, not for half a century now have sailors from Italian grain ships filled the bars of Taganrog. Events in Italy and Russia have dictated (an appropriate word) otherwise. Mussolini set out to make Italy self-sufficient, and,

Opposite: Pasta comes in hundreds of shapes and sizes. Nineteen of them are shown here.

Below: Beyond the macaroni curtain. Making macaroni in Russia fifty years ago.

as part of his "Battle for Wheat," another two million acres, many of them quite unsuited, were planted with wheat.

In Russia, terrible disasters, both man-made and natural, struck the peasants in the 1920's and 1930's, and among the worst hit regions were the fertile lands where the wheat grew best. As if it were not disaster enough that the famines of 1921–22 and 1932–33 led to the deaths of no less than five million and ten and a half million peasants respectively, Stalin's policies brought about a further decimation of the inhabitants of the Ukraine. His ruthlessly enforced collectivization involved the destruction between 1928 and 1930 of up to three million of the kulaks — the better-off farmers who had been the backbone of the wheat cultivation.

Durum Today

Today a major source of durum wheat lies in the wide, dry and sunny plains of North Dakota and Manitoba. The grain from there is not only used on the American continent, it is also shipped to pasta manufacturers around the world. Expert buyers, who will compare their choosing and judging of durum grain to the wine maker's choice of grapes, can detect a difference between the grain from one farm and another.

Meanwhile durum wheat is still grown in Russia and in Mediterranean countries, with Italy remaining the major European producer. But then that's not surprising for a country that is far and away the largest consumer of durum wheat in the world.

Making pasta
-then and now

As with most things about pasta, there is a pleasing simplicity about how it is made. In essence, the grain of durum wheat is ground, the resulting semolina is mixed with water to make a paste, the paste is formed into the required shape and then it is dried. There are, of course, many refinements and subtleties, but these basic processes have been the same since pasta was first made and eaten.

Streams and Stones

Mills and grindstones seem to have been a feature of civilization since the beginning of time, certainly since man has eaten bread – and pasta. How many of the most beautiful houses in Europe are converted mills nestling in a green valley on a site where, from ancient times, the mill stream has been the source of power to turn the millstone.

In Italy, the grain was washed in the mill stream before it was ground. This was done by women who put the grain into wicker baskets, which they then plunged in the water. Then they spread the grain out on the slate threshing floor to dry in the sun, and while it was drying they picked out the stones and other impurities.

Once dry, the grain was ground between two large round grindstones, lying flat one on the other. The bottom stone never moved, while the smaller top stone, which had a hole in the middle, turned on it. The grain was fed into the hole, and when ground found its way to the outer edge of the lower stone, from where it was collected.

For grinding the much harder grain of durum wheat, the grinding surfaces of the wheels were ridged rather than flat.

Modern Milling

Today, the grains are still washed before grinding, but instead of wicker baskets there are carefully regulated jets of water. And instead of grindstones there are two contra-rotating steel cylinders. These, like the millstones, are ridged, with the ridges forming a spiral round the cylinders. The ridges, in profile, are saw-toothed, and as the cylinders rotate at different speeds the grains are sheared, rather than crushed, between the two cutting edges. The grain is then fed to further cylinders that are set closer, with finer teeth, until it becomes semolina of the required degree of fineness. However it will still contain particles from the outside of the grain – husk and pieces of bran. So, to clean the semolina, it is put through a purifier in which air is blown upwards through a vibrating screen. Fragments of grain that are attached to the husk get caught in the up-draft and lifted clear of the screen, while the cleaner particles fall through the sieve.

The end result is pure semolina ready to be made into pasta. Ideally it should not have far to go, so that when used it is still fresh, and indeed most modern pasta factories are close to mills – often linked to them – in a position where centuries ago there stood the original mill astride its mill stream.

Treading the Pasta

Semolina does not mix easily with water, but mixed it must be to produce the paste – or dough – from which pasta takes its substance and its name. Until about 1400, this slow process was done only in the home. In most houses, although not those of the poor, there was a *madia,* a large trough in which the dough was kneaded. (A medieval *madia* is now a much treasured and expensive piece of antique furniture!) After long and laborious kneading in the *madia,* the dough was slowly rolled out with a rolling pin on a large board, and eventually – when thin enough – cut into ribbons, or tagliatelle. *Tagliare* means to cut, thus tagliatelle are cuttings.

Slowly, over the centuries the production of pasta moved from being a purely domestic undertaking. A register of the artisans of Savona, dated 1577, lists men according to carefully graded levels of skill, from masters down to apprentices, occupied in making pasta. By the seventeenth century pasta was being produced on a fairly large scale in "factories." But the way it was made was certainly not what that word suggests to modern ears.

A common way of starting the process of mixing semolina and water was with the feet! A man would stand in the *madia,* and, holding a rope to keep his balance, he would tread the mixture, one batch requiring up to a day's treading. As people commonly went barefoot in those days, one could wonder if therein was the secret of historic flavors, never to be recaptured!

However this certainly was not the way the practice struck Ferdinand II, King of the Two Sicilies from 1830 to 1859 and notable despot, when he visited a pasta factory. He was shocked, and commanded one Cesare Spadaccini, a leading scientist of the time, to invent a better method of making pasta. At the end of a whole year's work on this royal project, Spadaccini had drawn up elaborate plans for a model pasta factory, the high spot of which was his answer to what he called "the abominable practice of mixing dough with the feet." Mechanization, as you may have guessed, was the essence of what he proposed, but a fascinating sidelight on how ways of thought have changed in the last 150 years is provided by Spadaccini's solution to the problem. For his new mixing machine replaced the offending Neapolitan with an elaborate mechanical man, whose feet of bronze – robot fashion – trod the pasta in the accepted way. This was thought an excellent idea, and the building of a great factory was actually begun. But then the king lost interest, the money ran out,

Braibanti

Agnesi

Top: Shining modern machinery for making pasta. Here spaghetti is going into the drying tunnel.

Bottom: In nineteenth-century Italy, a common way of mixing semolina and water was with the feet.

Top: *A* **madia**, *the wooden chest in which semolina was mixed with water.*

Bottom: *Museum pieces of pasta making equipment.* **Madia, gramola** *— for kneading the dough — and a press for extruding it.*

the factory was never finished, and feet of flesh and bone
went on treading the dough for at least another
fifty years.

Man-Powered Machines

All this treading only achieved the
first stage of working a carefully
regulated amount of water and
semolina together into dough. There
followed the kneading necessary
to produce a really smooth, homo-
genous mixture. Until the end of the
nineteenth century, and later in some
small factories, the machinery — or
perhaps one should say the apparatus
— for kneading the dough, and for
forming it into spaghetti, was powered
in various ways by men or boys. As
shown on page 18 a long pole or a wheel
were the usual means by which human
energy was transferred to the process in
question. The dough was kneaded by repeated
pommelling with the end of a wooden pole, or it
was crushed by a rotating stone wheel. It was then
put in a press, where a great screw bore downwards as
it was turned, forcing the dough under extreme pressure against a
perforated plate, or die. Forced through small holes, the dough finally emerged
as spaghetti. These machines were made mostly of wood (100 years earlier they
had been entirely so), but the oak press was lined with bronze, the screw and
plunger were also metal and the die was made of copper.

Sun and Sea Air

A notable part of the Italian scene for smart young Englishmen making the
Grand Tour in the eighteenth century was the spaghetti hanging out to dry in
the streets of Naples. Outside a pasta factory the street would be lined with
endless racks strung with spaghetti drying in the sun.

However, the drying process is by no means as simple as "drying in the sun"
makes it sound. If pasta dries too quickly it will become very brittle, if it dries
too slowly it will go rancid. So it must dry neither too fast nor too slowly, and
this was just what the climate of Naples made possible. Hot winds blowing off
Vesuvius alternated with fresh sea breezes and between them they provided
perfect drying conditions for the pasta. The fact that two towns near Naples,
Torre Annunziata and Gragnano, came to be — and still are — famous centers of
pasta manufacture was largely due to the beneficial effect of these winds in the
days when pasta was dried in the streets.

*Above: King Ferdinand II, called King Bomba after he put down insurrections in Sicily in 1849
by ferocious bombardments. He was horrified when he saw men treading dough with their feet and
had a leading scientist of the day invent a machine to do the same job.*

In the Shadow of Vesuvius

Modern industrial history could be said to catch up with this story in 1878. In that year, the largest pasta factory at Torre Annunziata installed a number of mechanical purifiers (a modest little machine by modern standards) with an automatically vibrating sieve. Each of these could be operated by one man, where previously five or six men had been needed to shake the sieves.

The reaction of the workpeople was violent. They invaded and wrecked the factory and burned the offending machines. Violence was met with violence. The troops were sent in, there were fierce clashes and fifty of the "revolutionaries" were sent to prison — some for as long as six years. But the approach of mechanization was inevitable, and the people saw that nothing they could do would stop it. When, six years later, the same factory mechanized all the main processes and reduced the work force by half, there was no organized protest at all.

Mechanization paid dividends since it meant that the factory could keep pace with a rapid growth in demand. Production increased by leaps and bounds, and twenty years later, in 1904, this same establishment was employing a work force of 3,000 people.

Agnesi

*Above: A **gramola**, dating from the seventeenth century, used for kneading the dough. The vertical stone revolves on its own axis, and at the same time is turned round and round the basin containing the dough.*

Below: A huge screw-press, man powered, forces the dough through holes in a die, so that it is extruded as spaghetti. Note the bowler hatted, mustachioed proprietor and the man — bottom left — fanning the press to cool it. In front of him the spaghetti can be seen emerging from the press.

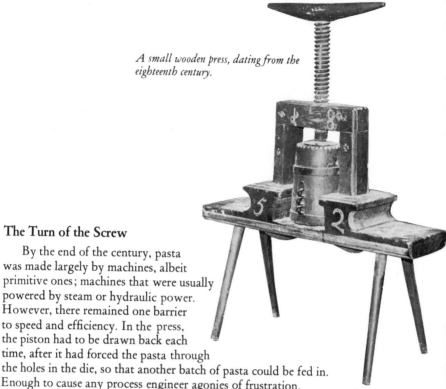

A small wooden press, dating from the eighteenth century.

The Turn of the Screw

By the end of the century, pasta was made largely by machines, albeit primitive ones; machines that were usually powered by steam or hydraulic power. However, there remained one barrier to speed and efficiency. In the press, the piston had to be drawn back each time, after it had forced the pasta through the holes in the die, so that another batch of pasta could be fed in. Enough to cause any process engineer agonies of frustration.

It was an ordinary workman, not an engineer, who finally saw a way around this block. Féreol Sandragné had worked most of his life for a Toulouse firm that made pasta-making machinery, so he knew the problem. When he retired, he took a job as a watchman in a brick factory to supplement his pension. There one day he noticed clay being carried forward and compressed by the threads of a helical screw, and as he watched, it turned to pasta in his mind's eye.

So he went home, and in his attic he made a working model of a continuous press for pasta in which the dough was carried forward in the threads of a screw, which then forced it through a die. Admittedly it got so hot with the friction that he had to put a wet cloth on it, but it worked, and it worked continuously.

It must have been a great moment for the old man when, in September 1917, he asked his former employers to come and see his model. They responded in fine fashion by taking out a patent in Sandragné's name and giving him a royalty on each machine they sold. And they sold many thousands in the years that followed.

Three dies, dating from about 1900, for the extrusion of long pasta.

Late nineteenth-century pictures of spaghetti drying in the streets of, top, Torre Annunziata and, below, Gragnano. These towns, near Naples, were the twin centers of pasta manufacture in Italy, mainly because the climate was perfectly suited to the drying of pasta in the open air.

Prince Macaroni

Prince Macaroni

Two views of modern large-scale pasta production. Top: Mixing the dough. Bottom: Elbow macaroni being extruded.

Modern Methods

This story, which began with the millstone, sees the start of its last chapter in 1933 when Braibanti (of the same family as the well-known pasta manufacturers) patented the first machine to include all the stages of pasta manufacture – mixing, kneading, extruding and drying – in one continuous process. Now we enter the era of automatically controlled production lines. The last stage of manufacture is no longer performed by the sun and sea air of Naples, but by automated drying tunnels, with hygrometers monitoring the moisture content to plus or minus half a percent.

Perhaps it is lucky that we shall never know just how that pasta tasted in Naples one hundred years ago!

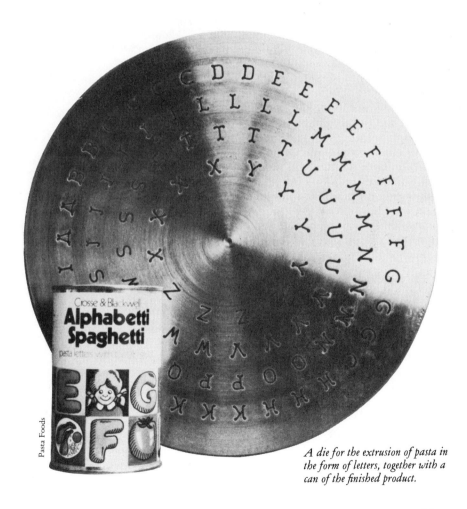

Pasta Foods

A die for the extrusion of pasta in the form of letters, together with a can of the finished product.

23

Pasta through the ages

The history of pasta eating is a fascinating subject. If its early pages are a little hazy, those telling of more recent times are full of glimpses into unlikely backwaters of social history. These may be less important than the main streams, but they are certainly no less amusing.

The Mists of Time

It seems certain that men have grown crops since the earliest traces of civilization, and that they were sustained mainly by eating the fruit of these crops. Indeed one of the reasons why most ancient civilizations were situated in river valleys, those of the Tigris, the Euphrates, the Nile and – in China – the Yellow River, was that these were the most fertile places where crops grew best.

These early people ate many foods that were made by crushing grains and mixing the resulting flour with water. In China, the Shang dynasty (1700–1100 BC) was the first for which a real and historic existence can be established. Already there was a fairly advanced civilization, and it is thought that one of their staple foods was a form of noodles. In that case our story starts almost 3,500 years ago.

The Greeks Did Have a Word for It

As we return from the Yellow River to the Mediterranean, still many hundreds of years before Christ, we pick up a definite clue. The Greek word *laganon* means a broad flat cake, made of dough and cut into strips, and it is probable that this dough was a flour and water mixture. Greek civilization flourished during the first millennium BC, so it is not at all unreasonable to deduce that pasta, in some form, goes back that far. Not only pasta itself, but also one of its many names, since *laganon* led to the Latin *laganum* – mentioned by Cicero, who loved to eat it – and thence to the Italian *lasagne*. And in Neapolitan dialect a rolling pin is still called a *laganatura*.

An Etruscan Tomb

The next piece of evidence dates from the fourth century BC, when Greece had passed its greatest years, and it was Alexander the Great who was striving

Above: Pasta manufacture in sixteenth-century Italy.
Below: A representation of pasta making utensils, carved on a pillar in an Etruscan tomb.

for the glory. Central Italy, west of the Apennines, was at that time ruled by the Etruscans, that mysterious people of unknown origin and undecipherable language. One of their main ports was Caere, about thirty miles north of Rome. All that now remains of this once important naval center is a large necropolis containing, among many other tombs, one famous for its bas-reliefs. These show everyday articles from an Etruscan home, and there on two central pillars are carved pictures of all the utensils for making pasta. These include a jug for drawing water, a knife, a rolling pin, a large board with a raised edge for keeping the water in when mixing it with the flour, a ladle for adding the water, a flour bag for dusting the board and a pastry wheel.

In many parts of Italy today, over 2,000 years later, you would find almost identical equipment for making pasta!

A Roman Taste

In one of his satires, Horace rebukes a friend, who is a judge, for not being able to go around the streets of Tivoli without five servants following him. For his part, he says, he goes where he pleases. "I wander through the streets . . . or often in the forum I stop at the fortune teller's. Then I go home to my supper, to a bowl of leeks, chickpeas and lasagne." (If you think that sounds good, try the recipe on page 118). Although the modern Italian for chickpeas is *ceci*, the Latin *ciceri* has been fossilized in the name *ciceri e trii* still used for a soup of chickpeas and fried tagliatelle in parts of southern Italy. (*Trii* is another revealing word, as explained in the next section.)

Only a few decades after Horace, there lived one Marcus Gabius Apicius, whose name became a byword for gluttony. Judging by the number of contemporary references to him he must have been a sensational eater. Having eaten his way through a considerable fortune, he could not face the prospect of the lean days ahead, and killed himself. Between meals he wrote one of the earliest cookbooks,

A Roman feast, with servants galore and the diners reclining on their couches.

De re coquinaria, and in this he refers to strips of dough fried and dressed with honey and pepper. Another suggestion is for pasta cooked in oil and dressed with pepper and *garum*.

Mention of this Roman ketchup prompts the reflection that although appetites do not change over the centuries, tastes certainly do. *Garum* was a sauce which the Romans seem to have splashed liberally on most things they ate – and it was made from the entrails of mackerels! It is hard to believe that we should find this to our taste, any more than we should some of the sweet and sour mixtures, such as honey and pepper, that were commonplace in Roman times, and later.

Arab String

The gluttony of Apicius was in tune with the times. Riotous eating was one outward sign of luxury and excess. While Rome indulged itself in what today would be called "an orgy of consumer spending," the outposts of its vast empire were being eroded by invasions from both North and South. From the South came the Arabs to overrun Spain, and later Sicily, and they brought with them a

culture that was in many respects highly developed.

In ninth-century Spain, under the Emir Abdurrahman II (whose son was to rule for 50 years over Spain's great period of Moorish prosperity) there was a famous Arab minstrel called Ziryab. A novel feature of his songs was that they often spoke of food, of its attractiveness, and of the elegance with which it should be eaten. And among the foods mentioned are several that seem to be forms of pasta.

At this time it was the Arabs who were also masters of Sicily, where their cultural influence persisted for a long time after the island was conquered by the Normans. This conquest took place within a few years of that other, better known Norman conquest at Hastings. The second Norman ruler of Sicily was King Roger II (1093–1154), and he commissioned an Arab geographer, Al-Idrisi, to write a book about his wanderings and explorations. In this Al-Idrisi says that at Trabia, near Palermo, he saw people making a food from flour, in the form of threads, which they called by the Arab word for string, *itriyah*. *Itriyah* became *tria,* and, as we have seen, *trii* is to this day a word for spaghetti in parts of Sicily and other places in southern Italy.

Giovanni Boccaccio. Macaroni is mentioned in the **Decameron,** *written about 1350.*

Marco Polo. He wrote of lasagne in 1300.

This use of an Arab word clearly implies an Arab origin for spaghetti, but who is to know whether this ante-dated the Greek and Etruscan pasta? What it tells us is that pasta was eaten in different Mediterranean countries from earliest times, and the probability must be that the origins in the different countries were independent of each other. Certainly this pasta took many different forms according to how it was cooked. The most usual was for the dough to be fried or baked, and then eaten dry or in a soup. Indeed, to eat pasta fried was quite normal until the sixteenth century, and even when boiled it was often fried immediately afterwards.

Medieval Macaroni

Some writers have said that Marco Polo introduced pasta into Italy, after his twenty years' stint as a sort of Secretary of State to Kubla Khan. This is a pleasing romantic notion, but unfortunately it does not square with the facts.

For there is a reference to macaroni in a document which dates from 1279, sixteen years *before* Marco Polo arrived back in Venice. In this 700 year-old document, which is in the Genoa city archives, there is a notary's list of the items left on his death by one Ponzio Bastone. Among these there figures a "*bariscella piena de macaronis,*" a basket full of macaroni. The contents of this basket are interesting for two reasons. First, this is the earliest known reference to what must have been dried pasta, as we know it now; secondly the fact that the macaroni was separately listed by the notary is an indication that it was something of a luxury, rather than an everyday dish.

Marco Polo tells of many strange things he saw in the East, although Sumatra seems to have had more than its fair share. He describes how, in one part of the island, if someone was due to die "men come and put something over his mouth to suffocate him. When he is dead, they cook him. Then all his kinsfolk assemble and eat him whole." As if that was not too out of the ordinary, he goes on: "Now here is something really remarkable. I give you my word that in this kingdom there are men who have tails as thick as a dog's." And the next marvel he describes is the one that gives him a place in this story: flour made from trees.

The Sago Palm is still an oddity – the tree with the soft center. Marco Polo describes how this starchy pith was mixed with water and the sago flour extracted (much as it is today) to make bread and cakes and also "lasagne which are very good and which I often ate."

The next medieval macaroni marvel is a great high mountain of grated Parmesan. In Boccaccio's *Decameron,* one of the stories is of the gulling of a simple soul. He is called Calandrino, and because he is simple his friends like to play tricks on him. So they tell him of some magic black stones he must collect in vast quantity and take home to his wife. (You can imagine his wife's reaction, when the poor man eventually arrives home, weary and weighed down with black stones!) To whet his appetite they describe a far-off place where the stones are to be found. There "on a mountain, all of grated Parmesan cheese, dwell folk that do nought else but make macaroni and ravioli, and boil them in capon's broth, and then throw them down to be scrambled for." Even in 1350 macaroni and grated Parmesan was something to tell stories about.

Francesco di Marco

By the fourteenth century, pasta had become a regular part of Italian life. Scattered through documents of the period are references, for example, to a shop in Florence where pasta was made and sold; or to two pasta makers from Rome embarking on a galley where they were to keep the crew happy with fresh pasta during the voyage.

However there is one particular source of information that gives a detailed insight into every aspect of Italian life at this time, including of course pasta. This lies in the incredible store of over 140,000 letters written by the merchant Francesco di Marco of Prato, and still preserved in his house there. No wonder that he once wrote: "I am not feeling very well today on account of all the writing I have done in these two days, without sleeping either by night or by day, and in these two days eating but one loaf."

One loaf was not his usual fare, however, as Francesco liked good food and could afford it. And, like many people who are reading this, he was particularly keen on the first course. This, as often as not, was lasagne or ravioli, and the stuffing of the ravioli consisted of pounded pork, eggs, cheese and a little sugar and parsley, after which the ravioli were fried in lard and powdered with sugar! Self denial during Lent consisted of eating special meatless ravioli that were stuffed with herbs and cheese and sprinkled with spices.

In the city-states, at that time, there were "sumptuary" laws which sought to restrain those with money from spending it too lavishly or ostentatiously. A banquet could only consist of three courses, but the Italians – then as now – were clever at getting around tiresome regulations. Thus the second course usually turned out to be a vast pie that was a gargantuan meal in itself. One such pie was made with chickens, sausages and ravioli filled with ham, which were laid on layers of pastry alternately with layers of dates and almonds, the whole being then covered with pastry and cooked in hot embers. And that, remember, was only the *second* course. Many things about man may have improved over the last 600 years, but not – apparently – his powers of digestion!

Renaissance Riches

The Renaissance was so called because it was a rebirth of the classical forms of art, particularly architecture and literature. In the culinary arts, too, Latin origins were studied again, notably by one Bartolomeo Sacchi. He had just been made head librarian at the Vatican, when in 1475 he published a cookbook that was to become a bestseller. Sacchi was a scholar, and the fact that he called himself Il Platina after the Latin name of his home town Piadena is an indication of his love of the days of ancient Rome. His book *De Honesta Voluptate ac Valetudine (Of Honest Pleasure and Well-Being)* drew considerably from Apicius and from other classical writers. A remarkable sign of the great interest that there must have been in cooking in Renaissance Italy is the fact that between 1475 and 1500 *De Honesta Voluptate* went to nine editions, a large number for those days. Il Platina included many recipes for pasta, in one of which he specified that the pasta should be cooked "for as long as it takes to say three Pater Nosters."

Opposite: Left: Bartolomeo Sacchi, known as Il Platina. His cookbook, published in 1475, ran to nine editions by 1500.
Right: Catherine de Medici married the heir to the French throne in 1533. As Queen of France she served her native pasta to the French nobility.

Below: Despite the size of the banquets, there was energy left for music and dancing afterwards.

The three-course feasts given by the merchant of Prato would probably seem like light meals compared to the vast and elaborate banquets given in the days of the Renaissance and after by the great families of Italy in their splendid palaces. In Rome the Dorias, in Ferrara the Estes, in Mantua the Gonzagas, in Milan the Viscontis and the Sforzas, and last but by no means least – in Florence the Medicis. When Lorenzo the Magnificent was married, he lived up to his name by giving a banquet a day for five consecutive days. Indeed, as even French historians will admit, Italian cooking was far and away the most highly developed in Europe at this time. Thus when Catherine, the fourteen-year-old great granddaughter of Lorenzo, married the heir to the French throne in 1533, it was natural that she should take her Italian cooks to France with her. Fourteen was not so young for a bride then, and certainly old enough for her to have acquired in Florence the taste for extravagance and beauty. This she took with her to the French court, and in the new palace at Fontainebleau, in the Tuileries palace that she had just built, as well as in her other Paris pied-a-terre, the Louvre, Catherine gave sumptuous banquets *à l'Italienne*. At these her expatriate Florentine cooks often served pasta to the nobility of France. However the French never took Catherine de Medici to their hearts, which is not surprising considering her propensity to have her political enemies murdered in large numbers, nor did they adopt her national dish.

A Closed Shop for Pasta

By 1400 pasta had ceased to be a purely homemade product and was being made commercially for sale. Like bread, pasta was sold in special shops and was made in the room behind the shop. As *vermicelli* was the usual generic word for pasta until the eighteenth century, a man who made pasta was a *vermicellaio,* and the shop he sold it in was the *bottega di vermicellaio.* The large room at the back contained the *madia,* in which the dough was kneaded, and the screw press for extruding it, and between there and the shop there was a courtyard for drying the pasta. In addition, so a contemporary document tells us, there was a bedroom for the night watchman.

The need for a night watchman is a reminder of the fact that in the Renaissance period pasta was still far from cheap. It was eaten by the rich, and for the mass of ordinary people it was for feast days, weddings and other special occasions. As the manufacture of pasta became a trade of some importance, so – in those days when the state intervened in so many details of daily life – its price was controlled by law. There are many records of proclamations issued in the various cities of Italy in the fifteenth and sixteenth centuries which specified the exact price per pound at which particular forms of pasta could be sold. It is interesting to compare the official price of 40 centimes for the equivalent of a kilogram of pasta in Naples in 1670, with the official price of 400 lire for the same amount in October 1974. Perhaps one thousand-fold inflation in three hundred years should not surprise us too much!

It was not until about a hundred years after pasta was first made commercially that the *vermicellai* began to band together into *arti,* or guilds. They did so mainly to protect their interests against those of the bakers. The main point at issue was whether bakers should be allowed to go on making and

BANDO
CONTRA VERMICELLARI.

 Olendo l'Illustrisſimi Signori Conſeruatori della Camera di Roma, conforme alla mente di N. S. prouedere che il publico non ſia aggrauato da Vermicellari, & altri, nel comprare da loro, ſi è riſoluto con Monſig. Illuſtriſs. & Reuerendiſs. Cardinale Camerlengo, che all'arti ſi manda il particolar Bando, non oſtante il generale; acciò li compratori con più facilità, & diſtintamente poſſano vedere li prezzi delle ſotto- ſcritte robbe, e conforme a detti prezzi pagare. Però commandano per il preſente publico Bã- do a Vermicellari di Roma, che dalla publicatione d'eſſo in poi, debbiano oſſeruare inuiolabil- mente li ſottoſcritti prezzi, e Capitoli. Auuertendo ad ogn'vno, che contra li diſobedienti ſi pro- cederà con ogni rigore, con Corda, Berlina, Fruſta, e Galera, & altre pene.

Pane bianco buono , ben cotto , & con ditio ſato, oncie ſette baiocco	1.		
Laſagne à vento , la libra	baiocchi	3.	quattrini 4.
Vermicelli gialli , la libra	baiocchi	3.	quattrini 4.
Vermicelli , e Tagliolini bianchi , la libra	baiocchi	3.	quattrini 2.
Maccaroni bianchi , e delli più belli , la libra	baiocchi	3.	quattrini 2.
Laſagne ordinarie , la libra	baiocchi	3.	
Conciatura buona , lo ſcorzo	baiocchi	13.	
Semola , lo ſcorzo per	baiocchi	5.	
Et di mezzo ſcorzo	baiocchi		quattrini 12.
Pane paſtoreccio , la decina	baiocchi	14.	

1 Li Vermicellari, debbano dare al compratore le ſudette robbe à prezzi ſudetti; ſotto pena di ſcudi 25. e tre tratti di corda in ogni caſo di contrauentione, d'applicarſi ſecondo il ſolito.

2 Item, che debbiano di continuo tenere nelle loro botteghe in moſtra le ſudette robbe, & in par ticolare delli Vermicelli, & Tagliolini bianchi; ſotto pena di ſcudi 25. di tre tratti di corda, & pene contenute nel Bando generale, & altre pene, ad arbitrio de' Signori Conſeruatori.

3 Item debbiano tener il preſente Bando incollato in vna tàuoletta nelle loro botteghe; ſotto pe- na d'vno ſcudo, & in vn'altra tauoletta il Bando generale; ſotto la ſudetta pena.

4 Item ſi dechiara, che nelle coſe quì non eſpreſſe s'habbi à ſtare alla dechiaratione dell' Illuſtriſ- ſimi Signori Conſeruatori, e contra li traſgreſſori ſi procederà conforme alle pene del Ban- do generale, di corda, berlina, fruſta, e galera inuiolabilmente ſenz' alcuna remiſſione.

5 Item ſi dichiara, acciò ſiano detti prezzi oſſeruati, che non ſolo ſi darà fede alli Signori eſtraor- dinarij maggiori, e minori : ma ad vn ſolo compratore con il giutamento. Dat. di Campi- doglio li 14. d' Ottobre 1602.

Simone Petronio Conſeruatore.
Ceſare Thedallino Conſeruatore.
Gaſparo Ruggieri Conſeruatore.

Io. Thomas Piuzzellus Scriptor DD. Conſer.

Ib Domenico Trombetta, e compagni, habbiamo publicato il preſente Bando nelli lochi ſoliti, e conſueti, queſto di 14. d'Ottobre 1602.

IN ROMA, Appreſſo gli Stampatori Camerali. M. DCII.

1602.

Agnesi

A proclamation issued in Rome in 1602, specifying the exact prices at which bread and pasta must be sold. Penalties for disobedience include a fine, three lashes of the whip and the threat of prison.

selling pasta, something to which the *vermicellai* objected vigorously. The controversy, which at times was nearer a battle, rumbled and raged throughout Italy — with occasional enforced truces — through the fifteenth, sixteenth and seventeenth centuries. At one stage, in 1608, the Pope intervened and issued a decree saying that bakers in Rome who wished to sell pasta must come under the guild of the *vermicellai,* and vice versa. When this carefully balanced judgement failed to stop the struggle, a later Pope came down on the side of the *vermicellai* by ruling that bakers who made pasta would be punished by a fine and three lashes of the whip. Even this did not stop the bakers, whose strength lay in the difficulty of administering three lashes of the whip daily to scores of bakers throughout Rome.

Slowly, however, the *vermicellai* won out, and an early sign of their increasing success and popularity was a Papal ruling in 1641 that there must be at least 25 yards between one pasta shop and the next!

Harlequinades and Odes

It was another *arte,* this time the actors' guild or *Commedia dell'Arte,* who gave pasta its first appearance, and at the same time its longest run, on the Italian stage. In their improvised plays, so popular in Italy in the sixteenth, seventeenth and early eighteenth centuries, the masked actors impersonated the familiar characters of Harlequin, Columbine or Pantaloon, each with their stock phrases and stock actions. Prominent among the well known and well loved figures was Pulcinella, one of the servants or *zanni* (origin of the English "zany").

Pulcinella's black mask had a hook nose, and he was a witty rogue as well as a practical joker. There was one thing that he seemed to be serious about, however, for whenever he appeared on stage he was eating voraciously with his hands from a steaming bowl of macaroni. He seems to have shed this habit in the course of his transformation into the English Punch, gaining instead a hump back, but retaining his special breed of jolly villainy.

It was not to be thought that a people so given to song as the Italians would fail to sing the praises of pasta. One of the first to do so was the seventeenth-century Neapolitan poet, Scruttendio. In 1646 he wrote an elaborate mock-heroic epic about pasta entitled *In Praise of Macaroni.* In a far more relaxed vein he wrote a sweet little poem to his beloved, Cecca, from which the following is one verse.

> *Me deze no piatto Ceccarella*
> *de cierte sapurite maccarune,*
> *semmenate de zuccaro e cannella,*
> *cosa da far sparire le pperzune.*

For those whose seventeenth-century Neapolitan is not up to scratch, here is a loose translation:

> My dear little Cecca, she gave me a plate
> Of macaroni delicious with a taste that was great.
> All sprinkled with sugar and cinnamon round about,
> So good when I ate it I almost passed out.

Pulcinella, stock figure of the
Commedia dell'Arte, *usually*
appeared on stage carrying his bowl
of pasta.

Naples Supreme

So we reach the eighteenth century, when the story of pasta, until now somewhat episodic, is about to sweep to its grand climax. Yet for some fifty years more the hero was to wait in the wings, for until about the middle of the eighteenth century Naples was known as the city of *mangiafoglie* – leaf eaters. It was the Sicilians who, in the seventeenth century, had been the *mangiamaccheroni* – the macaroni eaters, and they had scornfully given the Neapolitans the name that came from their love of salads and green vegetables.

By the late eighteenth century, however, this love of leaves was to give way to the grand passion that ruled in Naples for 150 years, and that is indeed still a contented marriage. In 1700 there were 60 pasta shops in Naples, and in 1785 there were 280. Along with Vesuvius, pasta became the symbol of Naples. This was partly because, in this city where life has always been lived very much in the streets, pasta was a public spectacle. It was hung up to dry in the streets, it was cooked in the streets, and – most remarkable of all – it was eaten in the streets.

There were the long racks festooned with pasta, gently drying as the hot winds from Vesuvius alternated with the fresh breezes from the sea. If the racks outside the macaroni maker's establishment tended to be tucked away in side streets, not so the *maccheronaro* – the macaroni seller. There he was, at many a street corner, his rotund figure giving ample evidence of the nutritional benefits of his wares, standing at his stall behind a charcoal stove and sheltered by a makeshift awning. On the fire was a wide, shallow pan (still the best shape for cooking pasta) full almost to the brim with boiling water and macaroni. At his elbow was a gleaming white mountain of grated Romano cheese, often topped by a small red flower or a tomato, and next to this a pile of plates. It was with his fingers that he served the pasta onto the plates, and it was with *their* fingers that his customers ate it.

36

Naples in the eighteenth century.

This is the characteristic Neapolitan scene, shown time after time in drawings of the period. A man, usually barefoot, stands next to the *maccheronaro,* his right arm raised, his fingers holding the pasta so that the lower end drops neatly into his upturned mouth. This everyday event in the life of the ordinary Neapolitan people soon became a tourist sight. Supercilious young English milords, doing the Grand Tour with their tutor and chaplain, came to see the *mangiamaccheroni* eating pasta with their hands in the streets of Naples. Anyone familiar with the entrepreneurial spirit of the Neapolitans will not be surprised to read that the *mangiamaccheroni* were always ready to demonstrate their technique for the price of a plate of pasta purchased by the watching tourist.

Late in the nineteenth century, and up to the time of the first world war, the production of pasta in the Naples area grew into what, for those days, was a giant industry. In the nearby towns of Torre Annunziata and Gragnano, where the manufacture of pasta was centered, there was a spaghetti boom. On the coast at Torre Annunziata the ships from Russia discharged their cargos of durum grain to be made into the pasta that was known throughout Italy as the best.

At the very same time, from the port of Naples itself, very different ships were sailing to New York loaded — and in many cases cruelly overloaded — with emigrants. Among the sparse belongings of all but the poorest families were several boxes of pasta, so that at least this reminder of home could help them face a new life in a strange country. Hundreds of thousands of these new Americans kept the spaghetti boom going in Naples, not only by the boxes they took with them, but by the even greater quantity that was exported to meet their needs after they arrived. And on almost every box was a label that reassured them that this was pasta as they knew it: a label bearing a picture of the bay of Naples, with Vesuvius rising above it topped by its plume of smoke.

Overleaf:
The macaroni sellers of Naples line
up to have their photograph taken.
The picture dates from about 1890.
Braibanti

Hands or Forks

The eighteenth-century tourist who watched in wonder as the Neapolitans eased the pasta down their throats would have been surprised to have been told that it was the Italians who, at least 200 years earlier, had been the first in Europe to use forks. There are a number of travelers' surprised comments about this. One of the earliest of these was made by a Frenchman who in 1518 attended a banquet given by the Doge in Venice. "The noblemen" he reports "when they wish to eat, take the meat with a silver fork." In 1605 an English traveler writes: "At the table they touch no meate with the hand, but with a forke made of silver or of other metall." Another wrote in 1611: "I observed a custome that is not used in any other country that I saw in my travels, neither doe I think that any other nation of Christendome doth use it, but only Italy. The Italians doe alwaies at their meales use a little forke when they cut their meat. This forme of feeding I understand is generally used in all places of Italy. The reason of this curiosity is because the Italian cannot by any means indure to have his dish touched with fingers, seeing all mens fingers are not alike cleane."

Perhaps it is fitting that the Italians who introduced the fork should have been the ones who later abandoned its use to such good effect.

Travelers' Tales

Italy, naturally enough, has always been a magnet for travelers. Sprinkled through the notebooks, diaries and jottings that they wrote are occasional references to pasta.

An eighteenth-century traveler from England was Hester Piozzi, better known as Dr. Johnson's great friend Mrs. Thrale. It is interesting to note in passing that Dr. Johnson himself only made one brief visit to the Continent,

Radio Times Hulton Picture Library

Above: The macaroni seller with his customers.

Opposite: His clothes may be in tatters, but one of life's main pleasures is still relished by this early nineteenth-century Neapolitan.

Dr. Johnson's friend Mrs. Thrale, who traveled to Italy after marrying her music master Signor Piozzi.

*Edward Lear, author of **The Book of Nonsense**, wrote of his Italian travels in the 1850's.*

when in 1775 he went to Paris with Mr. and Mrs. Thrale. It was ten years later that she went to Italy, but in the previous year, she now being a widow, "Dr. Johnson had the mortification [Boswell writes] of being informed by Mrs. Thrale, that 'what she supposed he never believed' was true; namely, that she was actually going to marry Signor Piozzi, an Italian musick master. He endeavored to prevent it; but in vain." In her journal *Glimpses of Italian Society* Hester Piozzi wrote of a Neapolitan prince who seems to have captured her fancy. "He shoots at the birds, dances with the girls, eats macaroni and helps himself with his fingers, and rows with the watermen in the bay."

Our next traveler is Edward Lear, known for his nonsense verse, although he would have liked to have been known mainly as a painter. In 1852 he traveled as far south as Southern Calabria, which not many Englishmen did at that time. In the journal he published he records an unusual incident which happened while he was dining with the Caristò family at Stignano (which is well down the toe of Italy). "A small juvenile Caristò, during the midday meal, climbed abruptly on to the table, and before he could be rescued, performed a series of struggles among the dishes, which ended by his losing his balance and collapsing suddenly in a sitting posture into the very middle of the maccaroni dish. One sees in valentines Cupids on beds of roses, or on birds' nests; but a slightly clothed Calabrese infant sitting in the midst of a hot dish of maccaroni appears to me a perfectly novel idea."

Andrew Peabody was a nineteenth-century Harvard professor, who himself had graduated from Harvard at the tender age of fifteen. In later life he traveled to Europe and, in 1868, wrote most charmingly about a journey to southern Italy. "On our sunset passage back to Massa (near Sorrento) the promises of a macaroni supper bribed our boatmen to sing. Their voices were both sweet and strong and it may have been happy for us that they *were* strong; for we passed very near the rocks of the sirens, and if those maidens have not deserted their dwelling place, we needed a powerful counterspell to drown their seducing melody."

"I left the maccaroni machine with my banker"

Thomas Jefferson was very much a Renaissance figure; he was the complete man. Statesman, philosopher, architect, writer, inventor — nothing was too great or too small to occupy his attention. And the interest he took in each of these different things was not just the result of idle curiosity. Viticulture or matches, clocks or writing machines, Jefferson applied himself as totally and as productively to these enterprises as he would be doing half an hour later to weighty affairs of state.

Food, and how it is grown, made and cooked, was a subject that greatly interested Jefferson. When he was in Paris from 1784 to 1789, he was constantly observing different European crops and plants and kinds of food. Pasta certainly came under this scrutiny, as is shown by his meticulous notes on how macaroni is made. Whether because of a fascination with the means, or a love of the end-product, Jefferson decided that he wanted one of these machines, and on January 22, 1789 he wrote from Paris to his young friend William Short, then in Italy, asking him to buy him one when in Naples. On February 11 Short answered, "I procured at Naples according to your request the mold for making maccaroni." We can then follow the stately progress of this strange machine over the next seven months, as it goes from Naples via Marseilles to Paris. Short is in Marseilles on April 3 when he writes to Jefferson, "I left the maccaroni machine with my banker to be sent on here to Mr. Catalan but it has not yet arrived, occasioned by the contrary winds which have been reigning now near two months." In fact it was four months later in August, when a postscript to a letter from Catalan in Marseilles to Jefferson reads, "I have lately received a box for you from Naples with a machine for maccarony, will you have it to Paris?" At the end of that month Jefferson answers requesting that the machine be sent to Short in Paris "by such sure conveyance by land as shall be cheapest." This, ten days later, Catalan replies that he will do.

This is the point at which this unexpected little backwater of history dries up. Did the macaroni machine safely reach the shores of America? Was it installed in the kitchens of Monticello, to be brought into use when Jefferson wanted a reminder of his days in Europe? We cannot be sure. It may well have returned to the States with Jefferson, who sailed from Le Havre in October 1789 and arrived back in Norfolk, Virginia after a near record crossing of twenty-six days. What we do know is that one of the amazing total of eighty-six crates that contained Jefferson's household effects — crate number 40 in fact — held a precious cargo: "two cases of maccaroni."

Thomas Jefferson, third President of the U.S.A. Jefferson became interested in how macaroni was made, and went to some trouble to import a "macaroni machine" from Italy.

How the *Mangiamaccheroni* Went West

Those two cases of macaroni were but the precursors of countless thousands upon thousands of cases, boxes and packets of pasta that were to travel across the Atlantic about 100 years later. During the early part of the nineteenth century, however, pasta remained – outside Italy – an occasional exotic flourish often added to rather elaborate menus to give variety.

Such an occasion *par excellence* was the banquet given by the Prince Regent, later King George IV, at the Royal Pavillion, Brighton, on January 15, 1817. On this occasion, the renowned chef Carême was in charge of the preparation of a feast which started off with four soups, followed by four kinds of fish, followed – as it built up to its grand climax – by four *pièces de résistance* (as they were known) that were surrounded by no less than thirty-six entrées. Here pasta made its modest appearance, one of these entrées having been *La Timbale de Macaroni à la Napolitaine*. This, you will need to know should you wish to duplicate the meal in its entirety, was macaroni and grated cheese, layered with force meat, steamed in a large mold.

In the United States during the years up to 1880 there was a small but steady

*Below: The Royal Pavillion at Brighton, where in 1817 a banquet given by the Prince Regent included among its myriad dishes **La Timbale de Macaroni à la Napolitaine**.*

Overleaf: December 10, 1906. Immigrants from southern Italy crowd on to the deck as their ship arrives in New York harbor. In that one year alone over 273,000 Italians arrived in America. Inset: East side meal time in New York, 1907. Living conditions may have been cramped, but for many they were luxury compared to what they had left behind.

Edwin Levick, Library of Congress/Lewis Hine, George Eastman House Collection

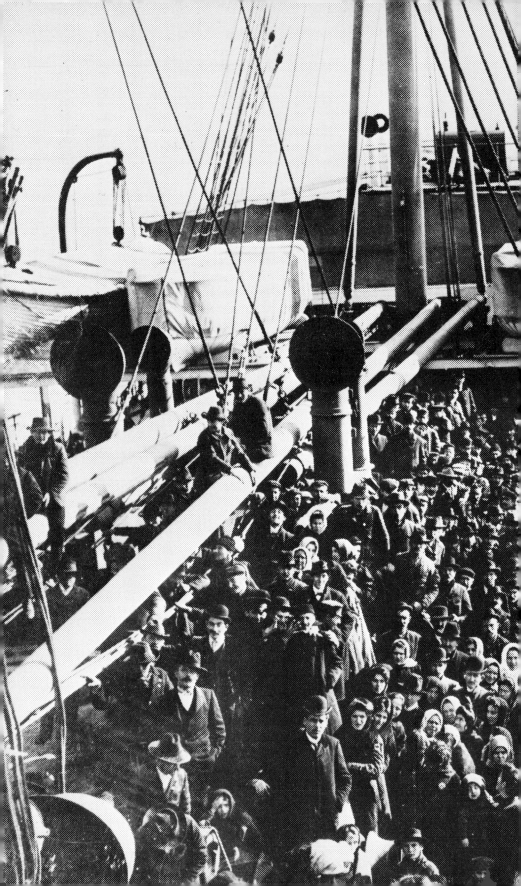

flow of immigrants from Italy. We get an idea of the conditions in which many of them lived from the writings of Charles Loring Brace, who worked so very hard to help poor immigrants in New York. In 1872 he wrote: "In the same room I would find monkeys, children, men and women, with organs and plastercasts all huddled together; but the women contriving still, in the crowded rooms, to roll their macaroni and talk excitedly."

However it was between 1880 and 1920 that Italy, as if from a severed artery, spilled out so much of its life-blood through the Mediterranean and across the Atlantic. The figures are amazing. In just those four decades, over four million Italians emigrated to America, nearly three million of them going between 1900 and 1914. They were mostly from the south, and in 1907 almost a quarter of a million came from the Naples area alone. The story has often been told of how the agents of the steamship lines swarmed over southern Italy, painting an alluring picture of high wages and a secure future. To reach this promised land, families endured atrocious conditions of overcrowding on board ship, sometimes being crammed in tiers three deep.

The start of the first world war in Europe had a dramatic effect on the flow of immigrants from Italy. The great wave of 1914, when no fewer than 283,738 Italians arrived in America, was suddenly checked, and in 1915 the figure dropped to just below 50,000. By 1919 the flow had become a trickle, with fewer than 2,000 Italians arriving. Then, the war over, the numbers surged again for one brief year, in 1920, before the first of the two immigration acts — in 1921 — brought the massive movement of the previous forty years to an almost complete stop. The second act, in 1924, ruled that only 2 percent of each country's foreign-born citizens resident in the United States in 1890 were to be admitted each year, and this curb struck particularly hard at would-be emigrants from Italy, since by 1890 only about 350,000 Italians had settled in America.

Made in America

It is not hard to imagine what a joy a plate of pasta must have been to these hard-pressed people. Newly arrived in a strange country, often desperately poor, a dish of spaghetti was one of their only links with the life they had left behind. Small wonder that they had no intention of abandoning the food that had been such an essential part of their old way of life, and small wonder that — as a result — the imports of pasta from Italy grew to what were for those days huge proportions. By 1914 imports had reached 77,000,000 pounds. Then the war brought a sharp and sudden drop in the imports of pasta — down to a mere 30,000 pounds in 1919.

This gave an immediate boost to domestic manufacture. Already a host of back-room factories were starting up, and these rapidly increased in number. Little family enterprises, using basic and very primitive machinery to knead and extrude the pasta, would find a ready market among their neighbors, who in all probability were from the same town or village in Italy. Only very slowly, through the 1920's, did the manufacture of pasta begin to catch up with the times. Families gradually began to come together to buy better machinery and manufacture in greater volume, so that they could sell to shops that were farther afield than the corner of the block.

One company, however, cuts across this general pattern and has a unique place in the history of pasta in the United States. For in 1848 a Frenchman, Antoine Zerega, had started America's first pasta factory, in Brooklyn. This was a factory the layout of which had evidently been planned with considerable ingenuity. Machinery on the upper floors was powered by a shaft that ran down through the building to the basement. There, in the basement, was to be found the source of power: one horse. The horse was harnessed to a boom that was in turn attached to the vertical shaft, and hour after hour, day after day, he trudged round, his energy being transferred to the mixing and kneading machines one and two floors above. The pasta, after being extruded and cut, was taken on to the roof, where it was dried in what was then, no doubt, the clear, fresh air of Brooklyn. Direct descendants of the original founder still run Zerega's, but they are now making their pasta in the slightly wider open spaces of Fair Lawn, New Jersey, and with machinery of far greater horse-power than was dreamed of in 1848.

Special types of pasta were made by hand – many hands in fact. This picture was taken in Buitoni's San Sepolcro factory in Italy in the early years of this century.

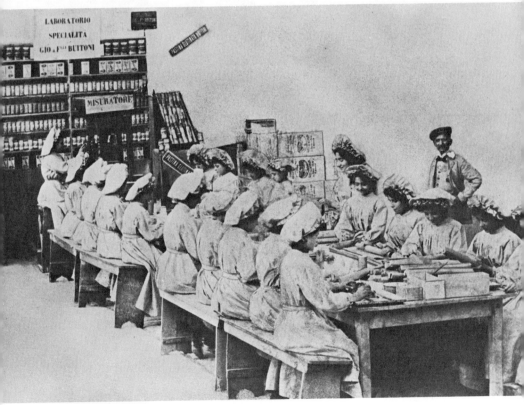

Buitoni

Who Was Mark Carleton?

With American production of pasta gathering momentum after the first world war, the factories had to be kept supplied, and so in their turn did the mills that fed the factories.

The chances are that not one in a thousand of America's pasta eaters have heard of Mark Carleton, and yet all of them owe him a great debt. Carleton lived from 1866 to 1925. He was an agronomist, working for the U.S. Department of Agriculture, who became an expert in plant pathology and, particularly, cereal rusts. Late in the nineteenth century, rust was causing great damage to the American wheat harvests. Carleton had already done a lot of research on the subject when, in 1898, he went to Russia to look for varieties of wheat that would be resistant to rust, and stand up well to drought. When he found the variety of durum wheat known as *Kubanka,* he was sure this was what he had been looking for, and he took quantities of its seed back to America with him. There, in North Dakota, only two dry summers were needed to prove him right.

Although he later introduced many other wheats to America, the successful establishment of durum seems to have been Carleton's particular concern. Not only did he publish two papers on the subject ("Macaroni Wheats" in 1901 and "The Commercial Status of Durum Wheat" in 1904) but he actually set out to convert everyone concerned, each link in the chain, to the cause of "macaroni products." First he visited countless farmers, to persuade them that planting durum wheat would save them from possible ruin, then he called on the milling companies to tell them what a future there was for them in durum semolina. Next he got food chemists to analyze pasta, in order to demonstrate its nutritional properties, and finally Carleton even sang the praises of pasta to hotel and restaurant cooks, and gave them books of pasta recipes which had been specially printed.

It was thanks to Carleton that durum wheat became so quickly established in America, so that in the decades to come the growing pasta industry had a good supply of home-produced semolina. It was thanks to Carleton that North and South Dakota, where 95 percent of America's durum is grown, were set on their way to becoming the rich grain-producing states they are today. Yet his name is not even mentioned in the *American Dictionary of National Biography,* and he remains an unsung hero.

Post-Depression Pasta

Although, in the mid-1920's, pasta manufacture was still a back-room industry, competition was getting tougher, particularly in New York, and the small family firms were jostling one another with increasing ferocity. The inevitable result was price cutting and, in the absence of adequate laws to protect the consumer, quality suffered. Egg noodles contained artificial coloring instead of eggs, ravioli were filled with meat of dubious quality, common wheat flour was used instead of durum semolina and you were well advised to weigh the packet that claimed to contain 16 ounces.

Then came the depression, and many of the smallest firms that had been struggling to stay in business finally went under. In those cruel days it was the

The end of an era. This photograph, taken in the 1930s, shows a kneading machine and, on the right, a press driven by wooden gear wheels. By the end of the decade a single, continuous machine for making pasta was in general use.

fittest that survived, so that the pasta industry as it emerged in the early 1930's was more efficient, and also more honest, than had been the case ten years earlier. However it was not only the raw forces of the marketplace that brought about this improvement in standards. One particular figure who knew the importance of pasta in the daily lives of one section of the community was Fiorello La Guardia. In the period between the two world wars, first in the House of Representatives and then as Mayor of New York City, La Guardia fought vigorously for the rights of the underprivileged and for social justice. Himself an avowed lover of spaghetti, La Guardia saw that the abuses being practiced by a few dishonest pasta manufacturers were also going on in other consumer industries. La Guardia's persuasive voice was added to many others, and was influential in bringing about the revision of the 1906 consumer protection laws. Far more stringent controls were embodied in the new legislation – the Pure Food and Drug Act – which finally came before Congress in 1938. Standards were laid down, and manufacturers were obliged to state on

Buito

New York, 1941. An eating establishment with the accent firmly on spaghetti.

all packages the place of manufacture, the ingredients and the net weight.

Through the 1930's the pasta industry expanded steadily. Larger manufacturers began to emerge, and to build their names — at least locally — through advertising. Pasta, now sometimes in a cellophane wrap, was no longer seen only in the shops of America's many little Italies, for spaghetti was ceasing to be a purely ethnic food. Pasta, like so many other European tastes, was becoming part of the American way of life.

Today, there is a modern pasta industry, yet it is by no means made up of a few giant companies selling their products nationally. For although 7 fairly large manufacturers command about half the market, the other half is divided between 114 companies. Of these, 70 are small local manufacturers who together only account for 20 percent of the market. So the industry is still relatively fragmented and regionalized, and family companies are the rule rather than the exception. Only about 70 manufacturers employ more than 20 people, and even America's biggest pasta company, the Ronzoni Macaroni Company of New

Associated Press

Fiorello La Guardia, mayor of New York City 1933-1941.

York, is still privately owned, with no fewer than 7 members of the Ronzoni family helping to run it.

In the last 25 years the consumption of pasta in America has increased dramatically. In fact it doubled from a per capita figure of a little over $4\frac{1}{2}$ pounds in 1949 to $9\frac{1}{4}$ pounds per head in 1974. This means that in 1974 Americans ate their way through 2 billion pounds of pasta. The only way to make this staggering figure dwindle into perspective is to remind oneself that in the same year, in little old Italy itself, they ate their way through half as much again.

La Storia Recente Della Pasta in Italia

In Italy pasta is politics, and in the 1920's and 30's in Italy politics meant Mussolini and Fascism. In 1926 a terrible *frisson* of fear shivered through Italy, when the story got around that Mussolini planned to prohibit the eating of pasta. What a bleak and terrible prospect! It was known that Mussolini wanted to cast aside much that was traditional in Italy, and the story was widely believed. It took party officials all their powers of persuasion to convince the frightened populace that it was a rumor without foundation.

Before long, however, another incident caused alarm and despondency. The poet Marinetti was the founder of the Futurist movement, as well as being an ardent Fascist, and he spoke with considerable influence. In 1931 Marinetti

A modern production line. Spaghetti leaves the drying tunnel before being cut to length and packed.

launched an all-out attack on what he called "the absurd Italian gastronomic religion." "It is necessary once and for all" he stormed "to annihilate pasta. It is something that is steeped in the past, a symbol of oppressive dullness, plodding deliberation and fat-bellied conceit." The shock-waves resulting from this pronouncement were felt even in America, where the National Macaroni Manufacturers' Association actually sent a telegram of protest to Mussolini. In Italy, they went on eating pasta.

It was Mussolini's "Battle for Wheat" in the 30's that was the beginning of the end of the ascendancy of Naples as pasta city supreme. As thousands upon thousands of acres of land were newly planted with wheat, in order to make Italy self-sufficient, the number of grain ships unloading in the bay of Naples steadily diminished. With temperature-controlled drying tunnels replacing the hot winds from Vesuvius, and with durum wheat being grown in central and northern Italy, there was every reason to build pasta factories nearer the big centers of population in the north. By the 1940's Lombardy was beginning to produce as much pasta as the area around Naples, and since then the relative position of Naples has steadily declined. In the last twenty years, two out of every three pasta factories in the south of Italy have closed down, and today Campania — the province of which Naples is the capital — is only the sixth biggest pasta-producing province in Italy. But though Naples can no longer claim to produce the most, she still claims to produce the best. They will tell you, in Naples, how some of the big companies from the north have opened a subsidiary in Naples just to be able to print on their labels those vital words *"Pasta di Napoli."*

Whether the pasta comes from the north or the south of Italy, the probability is that it will be of really good quality. One of the reasons for this is Law No. 580, as it is known. This law, which came into effect on July 4, 1967, laid down that all pasta sold in Italy must be made from durum semolina. Pasta made from the flour of bread wheat tends to go mushy when cooked, tastes less good and is also less good nutritionally. Such pasta is thus a thing of the past in Italy — as indeed it should be everywhere else.

In October 1974, the Italian government controlled the price of pasta, as part of their efforts to check inflation. There was an immediate outcry from the manufacturers that the price level fixed meant that they would have to operate at a loss. Until now, however, one has heard of no bankruptcies in the pasta industry. The price of pasta was first fixed by law in Italy about 500 years ago, and it does seem very probable that — in spite of the worst efforts of the government — those engaged in selling pasta to the Italians will manage to remain solvent for another 500 years to come.

Ice Cream to the Eskimos

Today pasta is made in many countries of the world, and there is a thriving international trade in the manufactured product, as well as in the durum grain from which it is made. As might be expected, Italy is by far the largest exporter of pasta — well over 130,000,000 pounds in 1975. Imports to the United States, although only $2\frac{1}{2}$ percent of the total U.S. consumption, have risen rapidly. In 1969 the figure was under 25,000,000 pounds whereas five years later, in 1974, it had doubled to about 50,000,000 pounds.

The strangest statistic of all, however, comes from England, where the local manufacture of pasta has risen to very considerable proportions for a country with a per capita consumption of only $1\frac{1}{2}$ pounds per year. About half the British-made pasta comes from the St. Albans firm of Pasta Foods Ltd., and they really hit the headlines when — in February 1975 — they started selling spaghetti to Italy. The headlines, in fact, were identical in England and Italy; they said: "*Spaghetti Inglesi!*" But this was not ordinary spaghetti, for Pasta Foods had shown great marketing finesse by approaching the Italians with a new kind of pasta, at a lower price. Pasta Foods call it "wholemeal" spaghetti —

... l'assalto alla Pastina Glutinata Buitoni !...

it is dark brown before it is cooked — and they make it from durum semolina that is milled in a special, and secret way. Whether the novelty, the price or just the sheer cheek of it is the attraction, the fact remains that this strange trade is thriving, and that shipments of this English spaghetti now leave regularly for Italy.

"A mere drop in the ocean" scoff the Italian pasta manufacturers. So it may be, but the fact that durum wheat grown in Canada, and made into pasta in England, can then be successfully sold to Italy is enough to show that future chapters of the history of pasta may contain quite a few unexpected twists.

*Italian pasta
packaging and advertising
from the early years of this century.*

Who Eats All the Pasta?

As the table shows, when it comes to eating pasta we are all dwarfs compared to the Italians. Even though they have been eating a little less in the last few years, the average Italian still gets through well over 1 pound of pasta per week. Somewhat less in the north, and therefore somewhat more in the south where it is quite usual to eat a dish of pasta every day. It would be interesting, for American readers, to be able to say how much pasta is eaten by Americans of Italian origin, but this little nugget of ethnic information seems never to have been dug out. No doubt it is well ahead of the American national average of $9\frac{1}{4}$ pounds of pasta per person per year, which works out at a little under a dish of pasta a week.

It is plain that Britain's pasta future lies all before her, as the annual consumption of $1\frac{1}{2}$ pounds a head means that the average Briton only eats seven dishes of pasta in a whole, long year.

A look at the *total* consumption produces some rather incredible figures. Italy still leads, but the United States (although its population is over five times greater) is not far behind. Britain, meanwhile, gallantly brings up the rear. The approximate figures for 1974 are:

Total consumption of pasta   Italy: 3,000 million pounds
USA: 2,000 million pounds
Great Britain: 85 million pounds.

Those with a fondness for silly statistics will be delighted to know that if all the pasta eaten in Italy in 1974 was ten-inch spaghetti, and if it all was laid end to end, it would make a string of spaghetti that would go 12,626 times around the earth, or to the moon and back 639 times.

The relatively high per capita consumption in continental European countries is due to the fact that pasta is usually eaten alongside the main dish, dressed with the same sauce as the meat or fish it accompanies. Japan has entered the lists comparatively recently, as only ten years ago no western-type pasta was eaten there at all. Now the annual consumption is nearly $2\frac{1}{2}$ pounds a head; considerably more than in Great Britain.

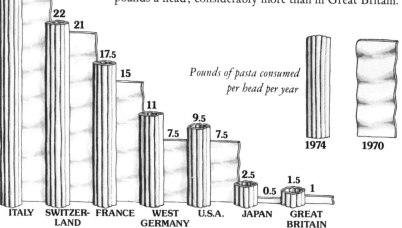

Pounds of pasta consumed per head per year

66 60 22 21 17.5 15 11 9.5 7.5 7.5 2.5 0.5 1.5 1 1974 1970

ITALY   SWITZER-LAND   FRANCE   WEST GERMANY   U.S.A.   JAPAN   GREAT BRITAIN

Pasta's many names

Pasta has not always been called pasta. Over the years it has had a succession of different generic names, in a way no other food has. Bread, after all, comes in many shapes and sizes, but the basic stuff is and always has been called bread. In English, bread is little changed from *brod,* which was the word 2,000 years ago, just as the Italian *pane* and the French *pain* are little changed from the Latin *panis.*

String and Little Worms

It is not surprising that, until their unification, the many dukedoms and principalities of the Italian peninsula spoke different versions of the Italian language. Some of the different words for pasta, therefore, were local names, although they would all have been understood from Milan to Naples. The word *trii* – the Arabic for string – was a name for pasta used in Palermo in the twelfth century, and still surviving in part of Sicily. Another very early reference to pasta dates from 1279, when one of the things Ponzio Bastone left his family in his will was a basketful of *macaronis.* And only a couple of decades later Marco Polo wrote about *lasagne.* Then in the *Decameron,* which Boccaccio wrote in 1350, we are back to *macaroni.* (See Chapter 3.)

In the fifteenth century *fidelini* was much used. This word is of Spanish origin, and is closely linked to *fideos,* which is still the word for pasta in Spain and all over Latin America.

Between about 1500 and 1800, however, there was one name for pasta in fairly general use throughout Italy and this was *vermicelli.* It is noteworthy that when John Florio wrote the first English–Italian dictionary in 1598, with the splendid title *A Worlde of Wordes or most Copious and Exact Dictionarie in Italian and English,* the two names for pasta that were included were *macaroni* and *vermicelli. Vermicelli* was defined by Florio as "a kinde of paste meate like little worms." No doubt some English readers wondered at a race that ate a dish resembling little worms. Florio, by the way, was the man Shakespeare turned to for advice about things Italian. He was the son of Protestant Italians who came to England as religious emigrés, and in 1578 he wrote a phrase book that was called, simply, *Florio, his first fruites which yield familiar speech, merie proverbes,*

*wittie sentences and golden sayings, also a perfect introduction to the Italian and
English tongues.*

Until the late eighteenth century, *vermicelli* was one of the two most
commonly used words for pasta. But by 1800, the word was *maccheroni*, and so
it was to remain for over a century.

The Many Meanings of Macaroni

If the foregoing paragraphs have told of many words with one meaning,
those to come are about one word that is remarkable because it has given birth to
so many different meanings. It all started because "macaroni" was essentially
Italian, and only Italian, and therefore stood for whatever Italy and Italians
stood for. Already in Elizabethan times, those who wanted to cut a figure and to
be seen as exotic would imitate Italian ways. In Ben Jonson's play *Cynthia's
Revels,* first performed in 1599, there is a superbly described character called
Amorphus, who is "a traveller. One so made out of the mixture of the shreds of
forms, that himself is truly deform'd. He walks most commonly with a clove or
pick-tooth in his mouth . . . he speaks all cream skimm'd, and more affected than
a dozen waiting women." Of Asotus, who was his companion, we read: "The
other gallant is his zany, and doth most of his tricks after him. He doth learn to
make strange sauces, to eat anchovies, maccaroni, bovoli [a kind of cockle],
fagioli and caviare, because *he* loves them."

If you made strange sauces and ate macaroni, you did so in order to tell the
world that you were a "traveller," and that having been as far as Italy, you were
well above the common herd.

Others, of course, might put a different interpretation on it, and by the
eighteenth century, when many more Englishmen went to Europe, those who
affected Italian habits came in for a considerable amount of mockery. This
scathing comment appeared in the *Oxford Magazine* in 1770: "There is indeed a
kind of animal, neither male nor female, a thing of the neuter gender, lately
started up amongst us. It is called a Macaroni. It talks without meaning, it smiles
without pleasantry, it eats without appetite, it rides without exercise, it wenches
without passion." This description seems to be inspired by a scorn of things
foreign, but the macaronies themselves were proud of their Italian connection.
They had formed, about 1760, the Macaroni Club, and this is referred to by
Horace Walpole in a letter. "The Macaroni Club is composed of all the travelled
young men who wear long curls and spying glasses."

For about 100 years in England, between 1750 and 1850, a macaroni was
any affected, overdressed person, in short, a dandy. But the particular affectation
of those eighteenth-century macaronies that most caught the public fancy, and
came in for the most abuse, was the wearing of fantastic wigs with the hair piled
high in truly amazing style.

It is those hair styles that cause the *Eudyptes Chrysolophus* to feature in this
story. For this is the zoological name of a species of penguin with an orange
colored crest, which is known as the Macaroni Penguin. I wonder how many
people have deduced from its name that the one thing this penguin really likes to
do is nibble at a dish of pasta.

THE FULL BLOWN MACARONI

Mary Evans Picture Library

In London in the eighteenth century a Macaroni was a dandy who wore an elaborate wig.

Look Who's Come to Town

Sometimes it was the coiffure, rather than the person, that was called a macaroni. And that is why, when Yankee Doodle came to town upon a little pony, having stuck a feather in his hat he called it macaroni. If he sounds a bit daft, and "doodle" meant someone who was that way inclined, this is because the song was first sung by the British to make fun of the Yankees. Then, when the colonial troops routed the British at Lexington, they sang "Yankee Doodle" mockingly at the British, and claiming the song as their own, kept right on singing it.

Finally one further addition to the harvest of words and meanings that grew from the eighteenth-century travelers' fondness for showing off their foreign habits. An early nineteenth-century dictionary of the Turf gives Macaroni Stakes as "those ridden by gentlemen, not jockies." Ridiculous they may have been, dandies they certainly were, but jockies . . . never!

Rude and Rustic

Pursuit of the word macaroni in all its meanings leads us to Mantua in the early sixteenth century. There we find Teofilo Folengo, who has been described as "an occasional monk." He did indeed become a Benedictine monk, but when he was only twenty-five he found the bonds of monastic life too oppressive, and soon afterwards he was wandering the countryside in the company of one Girolamo Dieda. He seems to have had a rare talent for getting the best of both worlds, since ten years later he was safely back in his monastery turning his literary skills to advantage with an account of his wanderings.

Folengo wrote under the pen name of Merlin Coccai, and his best known work was the poem "Baldus" which was a comic, and highly unmonastic parody of the poems of chivalry. However, what earned him the most fame, and a place in this story, was the language in which he wrote "Baldus," and others of his works. This was a cross between Latin and Italian, made up mostly of Italian words with Latin endings. The resulting mixture, which was designed to make the racy Italian sound like monkish Latin, was called by Folengo *poesia maccheronica* – macaronic poetry. It was, he said, a literary equivalent of macaroni, which he described as "a gross, rude and rustic mixture of flour, cheese and butter."

In more recent times, mixtures of Latin and English have been called macaronic. One example is the carol "*In dulci jubilo*, Now sing with hearts aglow." But such a mixture, not made with the orthodox ingredients, seems to be lacking the original macaronic flavor.

The New Name

Now all is standardized. Pasta is the word, and vermicelli, lasagne and macaroni are now just three of the myriad forms and shapes in which pasta can be bought. In English speaking countries, this has really only come about in the last ten to fifteen years. A book written as recently as 1957 comments on the lack of a generic word in the United States, and indeed "macaroni products" is the phrase still used by the American trade association – perhaps not surprisingly, as it is called the National Macaroni Institute.

In Italy the word *pasta* has been in general use for about fifty years, although the official phrase is *paste alimentari*. (No wonder this has not been adopted in English, since "alimentary pastes" sounds like some sort of intestinal medicine.) However, regionalism lingers on in Italy still, and certain kinds of pasta are local specialties with local names. When in Genoa you should ask for *trenette*, when in Venice for *bigoli* and when you are next in Naples you will make a deep impression on the locals if you ask for *strangulaprievete*.

Opposite: These are Macaroni Penguins, so called because their crests are reminiscent of the dandies' wigs.

Right: This handsome piece of wrapping paper is headed 'Paste Alimentari': the correct term for pasta in Italian.

Pasta people

A lover, a dramatist, two composers, two poets, two singers, a mayor, a novelist and a film star. Such is the list of famous people whose writings or sayings about pasta have been preserved.

The lover. Casanova needs no introduction. At the age of eighteen, not long after he was expelled from a seminary in Venice for immoral conduct, he stayed briefly at nearby Chioggia, where it is recorded that he looked so noble, and ate so much pasta, that he was dubbed the Macaroni Prince. To mark the occasion Casanova recited a sonnet in honor of macaroni, but sadly this has not survived. It is interesting, however, that macaroni should have been one of the early loves of so famous a lover.

The dramatist. Only a few years before Casanova was removed from his seminary, Goldoni was also a young student in Venice – but of a much more serious kind. However, one summer holiday, he and a friend met up with a company of traveling actors on a riverboat. Years afterwards, Goldoni recounted this incident in his memoirs. After telling how they spent a happy afternoon playing cards with the actors, he wrote "then the supper bell rang, and we all rushed to eat. Macaroni! Everyone fell on it, three bowlfuls were devoured; beef, cold chicken, veal, fruit, delicious wine: what a meal! what appetites!"

The first poet. Venice seems to forge a link between pasta and amorous activities. Several decades after Casanova's career was in full swing, we find Byron spending a few hectic years there, during which time he wrote Canto II of *Don Juan*. This contains a verse which suggests that pasta has hitherto unsuspected aphrodisiac qualities:

> Ceres presents a plate of vermicelli,
> For love must be sustained like flesh and blood,
> While Bacchus pours out wine, or hands a jelly:
> Eggs, oysters, too, are amatory food.

The first composer. Many of Rossini's happiest compositions were culinary ones, for he was a cook of some distinction. As witness the Tournedos Rossini.

Lord Byron.

Gioacchino Rossini.

He loved food, and of all foods he loved pasta best. There are several stories about Rossini and pasta, and various references to it in his letters. He wrote a letter, for instance, from Paris to a friend in Naples, the main burden of which was a lament that the macaroni he had asked to be sent from Naples had still not arrived. He signed himself "G. Rossini, *senza maccheroni*!!"

In 1815, the impresario Francesco Barbaia invited Rossini to his palace in Naples for six months, and there bestowed lavish hospitality on him, on the understanding that in return Rossini would compose a new opera, *Otello*. There followed six highly enjoyable months of Neapolitan pasta, wine and women . . . but no song. Not a note was written. So Barbaia locked Rossini in his room, and – worst penalty of all . . . but let Rossini describe this in his own words, as he writes to his devoted sister. "I have composed the overture to *Otello* in a room in Barbaia's house, where the baldest and most ferocious impresario has kept me prisoner, without any other pleasure but one dish of pasta a day, and with the threat of keeping me prisoner here until I write the finale." However, it was Rossini who got the last laugh. He gained his release by the simple ruse of

Radio Times Hulton Picture Library

Radio Times Hulton Picture Library

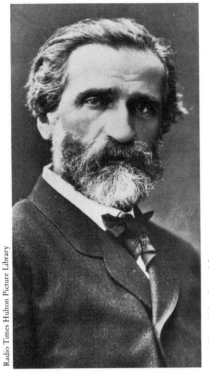

Radio Times Hulton Picture Library

Giuseppe Verdi.

Radio Times Hulton Picture Library

Enrico Caruso.

handing Barbaia four sections, marked Overture, Acts 1, 2 and 3, which – after he had gone – were found to differ only in their title pages, each merely containing the score of the overture, which Rossini had copied out four times.

An account of Rossini and pasta could not possibly end without a delightful tale which will be of great comfort to those who, like Rossini, find it hard to remember names and faces. A man sat next to him one day at dinner and said, "You remember me, I'm sure. I met you at that dinner given in your honor, when there was a splendid macaroni pie." Rossini thought for a long time, then slowly shook his head. "I certainly remember the macaroni pie," he said, "but I'm afraid I don't remember you."

The second poet. Alfred de Musset described Naples as that blessed land ". . .*où sont nés les macaroni et la musique*" – where macaroni and music were born.

The second composer. Verdi's feelings for pasta may not have been as passionate as Rossini's, but that is not to say he was immune to its attractions. Once, when he was in St. Petersburg in April and sorely missing the warmth of the Italian spring, his wife wrote from there that "it would take really perfect

66

Radio Times Hulton Picture Library

Mario Lanza.

Associated Press

Sophia Loren

tagliatelle and macaroni to put him in a good mood, amidst all this ice and all these fur coats."

The two singers. While Caruso and Mario Lanza are not known to have made witty remarks about pasta, both are known to have been inordinately fond of it. Caruso, when staying at the York Hotel on Seventh Avenue in New York City, used to give dinner parties at which he would cook the spaghetti himself, and dress it with superb sauces. And Mario Lanza once said that the one thing that really made him sing was spaghetti.

The mayor. Speaking to the United Nations about giving aid to countries in need, Fiorello La Guardia, made the only reference to pasta that has found its way into a dictionary of quotations. "Ticker tape" he said "ain't spaghetti."

The novelist. Mario Puzo, of *The Godfather* fame, once said: "Seven days without a plate of spaghetti drops me into a deep, dark well of physical anxiety."

The film star. Sophia Loren, when asked how American women could become as attractive as the Italians, answered: "They should eat more spaghetti."

Spaghetti fictions

Pasta, in a modest way, has its own mythology. Although this is not rooted in antiquity in the same way as is that of bread, there are a number of tales and legends about a food which – in one country at least – is as important as bread.

The earliest legend tells how Ceres, goddess of the crops, spurned Vulcan, who was the Roman god of fire, and how Vulcan took his revenge by stripping every grain of wheat from the fields. He then ground the grains with his iron club, plunged them into the bay of Naples, cooked them in the flames of Vesuvius and dressed this celestial dish with oil from the olives of Capri. Thus was pasta created, by a Roman god.

The Emperor and the Magician

The next legend is again set in Naples, and has a less remote setting in time. It is a legend that is still very much alive in Naples in slightly different versions, and the fact that they all contain references to an actual emperor indicates that there is probably some basis of historical truth in the story. The emperor in question is Frederick II who was crowned King of Sicily in Palermo in 1198 when he was four. It must have been a very small crown.

The central character in the story, however, is not the king but a magician called Chicco. Chicco lived in one room in a house in Naples, and he spent his days shut in that room carrying out curious experiments. No one knew where he came from and no one could decide what he was doing. When asked, he would only say that all he wanted to do in life was to make mankind happy. This, coupled with his striking looks, and his air of having once been a rich man, only increased his neighbors' curiosity. The more daring among them had managed to snatch an occasional glimpse into his room, and they swore that he was cooking something in a vast cauldron. Magic potions, perhaps? Or could it have been something far more sinister? Imagine, if you can, the excitement in the neighborhood when he was heard to cry out that he had discovered what all his life he had been seeking.

Now it so happened that the most curious and the most suspicious of his neighbors was a certain Giovannella, a lady of unsympathetic character who is in fact the villain of this tale. Giovannella was so curious that she used to spend her days spying on Chicco by looking through his keyhole, with the result that she — and she alone — had a very good idea of just what he *was* doing. It also so happened that Giovannella's husband was a cook at the court of Frederick II, who was now the Holy Roman Emperor. When Chicco made his discovery, Giovannella saw that her moment had come. She persuaded her husband that they could become rich by selling Chicco's secret, and pressed him to approach the Emperor. This he did, and Frederick agreed that his cook's wife should come to the palace and make this mysterious new dish for him. So Giovannella was sent for, and the servants in the kitchen were ordered to provide her with everything she needed. But all she asked for was flour and water!

The story goes on to tell how she made marvelous macaroni with a delicious sauce, and how this was presented to the Emperor, who was so delighted with the new dish that he ordered her to come to him. When he asked her how she had discovered this superb new food, Giovannella answered that it was by divine revelation. Then the Emperor sent his chef to learn from her, and he paid her a great deal of money for her secret. And after that all the nobles and dignitaries at court paid her money, and then the merchants, and then even those who could ill afford the price she asked for her recipe. Giovannella, on the other hand, was becoming richer and richer.

Of course it was not very long before Chicco chanced on someone cooking the new dish, and when he asked who had discovered it he was told an angel had revealed the secret to a Neapolitan woman. So appalled was he on hearing this that he felt he could not stay in Naples another day. Before night had fallen Chicco had left Naples forever, and no one knew where he had gone. What most people said, however, was that he had been taken away by the devil.

Meanwhile the years passed by, and Giovannella lived on, rich and seemingly happy, until one day she fell terribly ill. Then, as her illness grew worse and she lay dying, she confessed all she had done and appealed to God for forgiveness and mercy. Two days later, on a Saturday, she died. And ever since that day, Chicco has come back to the house every Saturday night. Then he is to be seen making his pasta, while Giovannella ceaselessly stirs the sauce, and all the while the Devil blows on the fire to keep it hot.

Miraculous Macaroni

In 1537 Pope Paul III beatified Guglielmo Cuffitella, who had lived his holy life in Sicily more than 100 years earlier. He thus became *il Beato Guglielmo:* the Blessed William. The process of beatification calls for evidence that two miracles have been brought about by the person concerned, and in a twelve volume book called *The Acts of the Saints,* published in 1675, we read that Guglielmo's two qualifying miracles were both performed in connection with a plate of pasta! There features also in both miracles one Guiccione, who was the blessed one's particular friend, and Guiccione's wife, who was a singularly disagreeable woman and not at all blessed.

Miracle the first. One day Guiccione invited the holy man to supper, having asked his wife to make ravioli. This she did, but with a difference, since to spite her saintly guest she gave him ravioli that she had stuffed with husks instead of meat. Guglielmo was not slow to notice what was up, but taking this in his stride, he made the sign of the Cross over the offending plate, opened a few of the ravioli, and exclaimed, "How delicious!" And behold! the ravioli were filled, not with husks, but with ricotta cheese.

Miracle the second. One Ash Wednesday, Guiccione again asked his holy friend to supper. But this time Guglielmo, knowing the difficulties that might result, said that he could not come as he was expecting a visitor. Whereupon the kindly Guiccione sent his little boy over with a dish of steaming hot lasagne. Guiccione's wicked wife seemed to offer no objection to this, but as she gave the boy the dish she whispered in his ear not to give the dish to Guglielmo, but instead to hide it in his cupboard. The days of Lent passed by, and Guiccione was more and more puzzled to receive neither his empty dish back, nor any thanks. In the end he sent the child to Guglielmo's house, and the child went straight to the cupboard where he had hidden the lasagne. He opened it, and there was the dish, piled high with the same lasagne, but — marvelous to see — it was steaming as if it had just been taken from the pot. "But, don't you remember?" said Guglielmo to the amazed boy, "you brought me the lasagne just now."

Blessed indeed was *il Beato Guglielmo.*

Overleaf:
This complex interchange of roads at
Gravelly Hill, Birmingham, England,
was quickly christened "Spaghetti Junction."
Birmingham Post & Mail

Opposite:
Gathering the spaghetti harvest in
Ticino, Switzerland. A still from a
TV documentary first shown in
England on April 1, 1957.

The Original Spaghetti Western?

An uncle of mine from Naples used to tell me a story that he heard, as a child, from his grandfather. It is a romantic story of love and intrigue, and it struck me for the first time, on setting it down for this book, that it might almost be described as a Spaghetti Western. For the hero of the story, Tommaso, was the youngest son of a noble family called Spaghetti.

Tommaso, at the time of the story, was in his early twenties, and although his life so far had been singularly free of care, things had recently started to go badly for him. He had lost a lot of money gambling, and as a result he was drinking far more than he should. Now he spent his time sulking in bars of dubious repute.

One sultry summer's day, as he was strolling down some back streets, the pensive young Tommaso was woken from his day dreams by a slipper which fell from a balcony and landed at his feet. He looked up and saw two pearly grey eyes gazing down at him. He was entranced, so much so that it was a little time before he realized that the heavenly face belonged to the daughter of that deadly family rival, the Marchese Tagliatella. So how could they ever meet?

Across the street, Signora Conchiglia had been watching from behind the bar of her café. She knew what was up, as she always did, and she called Tommaso over. "The Tagliatella's confidante is an old friend of mine," she said. "I will ask her to change clothes with her mistress, so that her parents will not find out that she is meeting you." And so it was that the two met in great secrecy the next day in Signora Conchiglia's garden. The talented Tagliatella, whose name was Giulia, played the mandolin, while her starry-eyed lover marveled at her beauty. Despite the risks involved, they went on meeting in the garden for some time, falling more and more deeply in love.

But it was not to last. The Marchese Tagliatella had betrothed his daughter to a rich and powerful ally, the immensely tyrannical Barone Rigatone. It so happened that the Barone's right-hand man, the Cancelliere Maccherone, was passing by one day when he caught sight of Giulia's confidante. Ever suspicious, he looked closer and saw that it was the mistress and not the confidante! And there, meeting her at the café door, was no other than the son of his sworn enemy the Conte Spaghetti. His wrath knew no bounds. He started shouting abuse at our hero, who, seeing he had nothing to lose, unsheathed his sword and made for his adversary. The fat Cancelliere was no fighting man, and he wobbled backwards toward the safety of the nearby Cathedral square.

No sooner had he reached the square than he bumped into the Spaghetti family's most loyal retainers, the wiry little Capellini who grabbed hold of him. Our hero arrived, and was about to plunge his sword into the Cancelliere's ample flesh, when there appeared the Barone Rigatone's secret dagger-men, the Lumaconi, closely followed by their accomplices in crime the Chifferi, and their relatives the Chifferotti and the Chifferoni. A quick summons to the other side of the piazza, and the Capellini had enlisted the help of their comrades the Vermicelli, who rushed forwards, all will-'o-the-wisp, to take part in the brawl. Everyone had some excuse for joining in, and the principal protagonists were all but submerged as the piazza became a battleground of the first order.

As a dagger stuck fast in its victim here, and a lance transfixed an opponent there, as stones flew overhead and spears whistled by to left and to right, night began to fall, and darkness soon covered the piazza. The final outcome of the battle, in fact, was never known for sure. All that is known is that Tommaso and Giulia were soon far away in the country among the olive trees and the vineyards, and rumor has it that there they stayed for the rest of their lives, preferring a simple rustic existence to the rivalries and jealousies of the life they had left behind.

No Pasta

". . . and the day dawned on which all Italy sat down to dinner without pasta." This awful eventuality comes to pass in *Italian Peepshow* by Eleanor Farjeon, a charming book of children's stories about Italy that was first published about fifty years ago in New York. There was no pasta because the crop had failed that year, and the young reader is left in no doubt as to the gravity of the disaster. Earlier in the story it had been explained that "Pasta is important to Italians" and this solemn statement is followed by a list of the different shapes and forms of pasta:

> Shells and
> Bells and
> Nuts and
> Apple-pips and
> Needle-points and
> Fleas' Eyes and
> Horses' Teeth and
> Holy Seeds and
> Olive Stones and
> Linen Sheets and
> Hearts and
> Diamonds and
> Feathers and
> The Virgin's Tears

When that awful day dawned on which there was no pasta, such a wail went up that it was heard across the sea by King Nero of Tripoli. At first he could not think what the noise might be, but fearing that it was the crying of men and children, he set sail and followed the cry across the sea to Italy. There, when he asked them, "For what do you cry?" they answered, "For pasta" and although one little golden-haired child ran away at the sight of his dusky face, he promised to try and bring them their pasta.

So he went to the sea shore and asked the sea for its shells, and the sea said, "With pleasure, if the church will give you its bells," and so the king asked his way right through the list until he came to the Virgin's tears. But the Virgin said she needed her tears to weep with. "The earth is angry with the fair child," she said, "and refuses to bear corn in her country until of her own free will the child kisses a black man." Then the King asked the Virgin for her tears so that he could weep in her place, and she gave them to him, and all the others then gave him what he asked for: the church its bells, and the sea its shells.

Then King Nero drove his golden chariot through Italy, scattering bells and shells and apple-pips wherever he went, and as they fell to the ground they all turned to pasta. At last he reached the village where the golden-haired girl lived, and as he entered the market square she ran out and gave him a kiss. At this the King beamed with happiness, and at the same moment the earth once again began to grow its crop.

Full of goodness

Most people love pasta. It is delicious and it is filling, and that is what they want their food to be. From this there tends to follow the conclusion that it cannot at the same time be good for you. Green vegetables and lettuce and fruit are good for you. Spinach, which as a child you probably disliked, is particularly good for you. But not lovely old spaghetti.

The logical application of this belief would be to eat only green vegetables and salad and fruit. Not long would pass, however, before you would feel weak, tired and very empty. You would become well aware of the real nutritive value of carbohydrates, and of the body's need for them.

The Body's Fuel

The three basic constituents of what we eat are carbohydrates, fats and proteins. A normal healthy balance of these three, expressed as percentages of the total calories provided, is:

Carbohydrates	60%
Fats	25%
Proteins	15%

As we get more than half our calories from carbohydrates, and as they are the largest single element in what we eat, they obviously are very important. There are many sources for the carbohydrates your body needs, and some are better than others. Pasta, however, is probably the best of them all.

One of the reasons for this is that pasta is among the most easily digested foods there are. It places no strain on the digestive system. Pasta is not only very easily, but also very rapidly assimilated, as it is quickly converted by the digestive processes into glucose. In this form it acts as a fuel for the body and provides abundant energy.

Vital Vitamins

Another reason why pasta is also such a health-giving carbohydrate is that it is in most cases rich in vitamins. All pasta contains vitamins of the B complex,

PRODOTTI SPECIALI

BUITONI

PER ATLETI E SPORTIVI

PANE E PASTA ALIMENTARE

La Ditta Buitoni invierà agli sportivi dietro semplice richiesta campioni gratuiti e prospetti illustrativi.

GIO: & F.lli BUITONI

SANSEPOLCRO (Arezzo)

This elegantly illustrated advertisement from the 1930's promotes Buitoni products "for athletes and sportsmen."

and pasta which is vitamin enriched (over three-quarters of the United States production is) contains these vitamins, and iron, at considerable levels. These levels are high enough to ensure that a 4 ounce portion of pasta provides the following percentages of the minimum daily requirements for an adult:

Thiamin (Vitamin B1)	50%
Riboflavin (Vitamin B2)	25%
Niacin	40%
Iron	32.5%

Vitamins are mysterious substances of which we need so little, and yet that little is so vital. It is easy to be blasé about vitamins and, because one hears so much about them, to assume that they are provided automatically. Yet only fifty or sixty years ago there were poor people in rural districts of the United States who, as a result of a diet based on corn and a little poor quality meat, were suffering from pellagra. At first, when their dogs were found to have a similar disease, it was thought to be an infection, and indeed it was only discovered in 1937 that it was a deficiency of the vitamin niacin in their diet that was causing pellagra.

The Right Mixture

Pasta contains proteins, as well as carbohydrates. Taking the pasta by itself, which you never do, it is about 12 percent protein. Proteins provide the amino acids of which your body needs a judicious mixture. Pasta contains the majority of the essential amino acids, and if you eat it with a meat sauce or cheese, you get an ample supplement of those others, so that the complete dish supplies an excellent balance of the total range of amino acids.

Pasta is a particularly low fat food, with a fat content of only 1.4 percent. This is especially important for those wishing to control their intake of fats, whether they are mainly concerned with eating less fat, or with avoiding saturated fats. In the latter case, an excellent answer is a dish of pasta dressed either with a plain tomato sauce (see the recipe on page 111), with olive oil (page 139) or with one of the margarines made with a high proportion of polyunsaturated vegetable fats, such as Flora in Britain or, in the United States, Fleischmanns Margarine or Promise. These margarines make a very tasty sauce – see the recipe on page 140.

A monotonous diet is not only boring, it fails to supply food in the way your body needs it. A recent experiment with rats illustrates this point. No, the rats were not given pasta! They were fed on meat and bread only, for a short time, and when these were given separately, with twelve hours between the meat and the bread, the rats stopped growing. But when the meat and bread were given together, they resumed their normal growth. Herein lies one of the main reasons why pasta is a food so well suited to the body's needs. Pasta, unlike bread or potatoes, is only part of the total mixture. One day you eat it with tomatoes, another day with butter, another day with meat and another with fish. All the different foods you need join with pasta to make the basis of a meal that is easily digested, nourishing and healthy.

Overleaf:
It's a question of total dedication to
the task in hand.
Radio Times Hulton Picture Library

Your figure's friend

"One of the least fattening cuisines in the world is the Italian cuisine: the real Italian cuisine consisting of a plate of pasta with tomato sauce, dressed with a little grated Parmesan, followed by a little meat or fish, a salad and fresh fruit."

Ancel Keys, Professor Emeritus of Physiological Hygiene, University of Minnesota.

You may want to slim, or perhaps you just don't want to get too fat. Either way it's simply a question of eating no more calories during the day than you are going to use up in body energy over the same period of time. It's as simple as that.

That's the theory. In practice, as anybody who has tried it knows only too well, it is not in the least simple. It is difficult, because if you tend to put on weight you are someone whose control mechanism, sometimes called the appestat, seems to be adjusted incorrectly. This means that nature, through the medium of hunger, prompts you to take in more calories than you expend. It is this excess hunger that is the culprit, making you eat that bit over the top – the bit that does the damage.

Something Satisfying

The reason that pasta is your figure's friend is that, eaten at the beginning of the meal, when your hunger is keenest, it quickly satisfies you. Even if you sit down ravenous, a plate of pasta quickly gets your hunger under control. You have eaten it with gusto, and your meal has already given you that essential feeling of reward and replenishment. Now you can be discreet. Quite calmly, without that sordid battle between your will power and your hunger, you can finish the meal lightly and sensibly. You will feel satisfied. You will have enjoyed a proper meal, rather than a miserable exercise in self restraint. Psychologically, you will feel refreshed, as you should after eating.

Counting the Calories

"And how," you may well ask, "can all this self indulgence possibly add up to slimming? What about counting the calories?" In fact it is very easy to count the calories with pasta, since you always weigh out a measured quantity before you cook it. The calculation is simple: 1 ounce of pasta = 100 calories. A normal serving, by no means skimpy, is 3 ounces, so that a plateful of pasta, without the sauce, gives 300 calories. To serve this pasta with a tomato sauce and grated cheese would add about 125 calories, while to dress it with butter and grated cheese would add, at the most, 100 calories. No more than 425 calories in all, therefore.

The average daily expenditure of energy for a woman is 2,500 calories, and for a man 3,000 calories. Thus a dish of pasta only constitutes one-sixth of a woman's correct daily intake of calories, and one-seventh of a man's. Correct, that is, if you are wanting to *maintain* your sylph-like figure. If you want to *lose* weight by cutting the calorie intake to, say, 2,000 a day (a reasonable quantity if you want to slim gradually) a plate of pasta complete with sauce, at 425 calories, is still well under a quarter of the day's total calories.

Keeping at It

Another reason why pasta has a particular part to play in keeping people's figures in good shape, or making them better, is that most people are not very good at mortifying the flesh for more than a few days at a time. The result is that grapefruit diets, and skimmed milk diets, and low protein diets, let alone diets based on special slimming products, are fine while they last – but wasted when they stop. For stop they do, and then the pounds come back – almost every time. A diet that you actually like, however, and one that costs you nothing extra, is a diet that you will live with quite happily for many a year to come. It is a long-term answer to the problem.

What better than a good dish of pasta followed, as Professor Keys suggests, by a little meat or fish, a salad and fresh fruit? At 750 calories, a meal such as this is the basis of a happy, healthy and lasting way to keep your figure the way you want it.

la linea

si mantiene con:

ANTOBÈS
BUITONI

la pasta e il pane che non ingrassano

GIO: & F.lli BUITONI · Sansepolcro
dal 1827 le migliori qualità di paste

"Keep your figure with Buitoni pasta" says the advertisement from 40 years ago.

Buying pasta

Pasta can of course be bought at most grocers or supermarkets, but if you are within reach of an Italian shop you will find a far greater variety of shapes there, and probably better quality pasta too. It is worth going out of your way to buy good pasta, as the difference in taste is quite considerable, and the difference in price is small.

The main thing to look for when buying pasta is that it must state on the package that it is made from durum semolina or durum wheat (semolina being to durum wheat what flour is to bread wheat). This is quite essential, as pasta made wholly or partly from bread wheat tastes less good and goes mushy when cooked. If the packet says nothing, you can assume the worst! All the exported Italian pasta is of excellent quality, but in America nowadays much of the locally made pasta is just as good.

Apart from what it says on the packet, you can tell a lot about the quality of pasta by looking at the raw pasta itself (although I cannot advise you to try opening packet after packet in the store!) It should be of a pale buff yellow color, rather than grey. When held up to the light pasta should be translucent — though you cannot see through the double thickness of hollow shapes — with dark specs visible within it.

After cooking properly, in plenty of boiling water and for the right amount of time (see "The five golden rules for cooking pasta" on page 100, or "A new method of cooking store-bought pasta" on page 101), good quality pasta will look moist, with every piece well separated. Also it should have at least doubled in volume. Good quality pasta, on its own, has a very delicate taste.

Shapes

According to somebody who once counted, there are 600 different shapes of pasta to be had in Italy, while Manganaro's in New York City claim to stock 500 different varieties. Of these about 50 are the common shapes that are more frequently found. There is some confusion about the names of these shapes, since different manufacturers (and in Italy different regions) sometimes give different names to the identical shape. I have included a pictorial chart of the most usual varieties, with names, so that there can be no doubt which shape is being referred to in the recipes.

With each recipe I have indicated the shape or shapes of pasta that are best suited to that particular sauce. If you want to use another shape – because you cannot find the one listed, or just for a change – the principle to remember is that long pasta goes better with tomato or fish sauces, while short pasta is best for a heavy, meaty sauce. This is because the short varieties are either convoluted in shape or hollow, so that they pick up more of the sauce and thus give the dish a richer taste. So it is usually best to substitute one type of long pasta for another, or one type of short pasta for another. However this is not to be taken as a rigid rule, since – for example – an excellent dish of pasta can consist of macaroni with Emilian tomato sauce (see page 112), just as an equally delicious dish is linguine with old-fashioned *ragú* (see page 111).

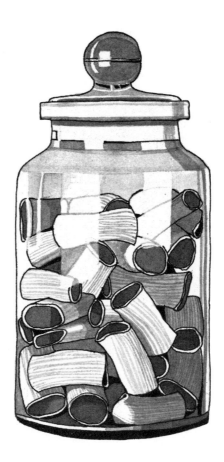

86

Eating pasta

The Rest of the Meal

Any meal must have a good balance of different kinds of food.

Pasta can be a first course, as it generally is in Italy, or a main course. This "one-dish course" has become very popular nowadays. The English and the Americans were, in fact, the first people to eat pasta followed only by a salad, cheese and fruit – a perfect meal if you want to keep slim.

If you serve pasta as a first course, the rest of the meal should be light and different from the sauce of the pasta. For instance: *bucatini alla carbonara* (see page 143) might be followed by steamed fish or veal escalopes with lemon and parsley; spaghetti with clams (see page 207) could be followed by ham and salad or a small steak with green vegetables.

Some of the dishes described in this book make a complete meal in themselves, e.g. *timballo di anolini* (see page 195), lasagne with cheese and mushrooms (see page 182) and nearly all the pasticci. These should be followed only by a green salad or some sautéed zucchini (courgettes) or spinach with oil and garlic.

It is very difficult to give hard and fast rules, since what you want to eat is up to you alone. It also depends on the occasion. A light supper could consist only of spaghetti with leek sauce (see page 147), but this would not make a lunch for hungry teenagers. What you should keep in mind is the balance of the whole meal, and the fact that each course should taste and look quite different from the one that went before.

What to Drink with Pasta

There are those who say that to drink anything other than water with pasta is profanity; others swear by beer. While I cannot subscribe to the water theory, there is no doubt that beer is a good accompaniment to pasta in most of its many guises. However wine is the perfect match for pasta – they might have been made for each other.

On the question of red or white, it is impossible to be dogmatic. It all depends on the sauce, of course, and there are a few sauces that demand one or the other. But on the whole pasta is very tolerant, and either red or white wine can be drunk with most of the sauces in this book with equal pleasure. I have not gone into the question of which red or which white wine, since this tends to involve long and tedious lists telling you to buy wines that are hard to find, or too expensive, or both. There follows, instead, a simple list with Red or White marked against those sauces whose taste definitely goes best with one or the other. The best way to take it from there is to experiment and to be guided by your own palate. The worst that can happen, after all, is that you will have the pleasure of trying again.

Recipe	Red or White wine	Page
Tagliolini with asparagus	White	146
Spaghetti with leeks	White	147
Spaghetti with caviar	White	149
Thin spaghetti with haddock fillets	White	150
Thin spaghetti with mussels	White	206
Short pasta with fresh sardine sauce	White	211
Trinette with *pesto*	White	191
Cold pasta dishes	White	162
Spaghetti with pizza sauce	Red	153
Noodle bows with kidneys	Red	156
Macaroni with pheasant sauce	Red	159
Elbow macaroni with sausages	Red	160
Stuffed cannelloni	Red	183
Pappardelle with hare	Red	196
Bucatini with salt pork	Red	201
Homemade pasta with hot lamb sauce	Red	202
Macaroni with *ragú* and mint	Red	212

Overleaf:
All sorts of pasta and Italian
delicacies at Olga's in London.
Dick Ehrlich

SPECIAL
OFFER

RECIPES

Conversion tables

The recipes in this book are based on American and metric measures. The solid American measures are ounces and pounds, equal to the Imperial measures. Butter, flour and a few other ingredients are given in American cups and metric measures. All metric measures are in brackets.

The liquid American measures are less than the Imperial Measures. In the recipes whenever "cup," "tablespoon" or "teaspoon" are quoted they are: American cup = 8 fluid ounces; American tablespoon = British dessert spoon; and American teaspoon = a small British teaspoon.

For simplicity, the metric measures have been rounded to the nearest figure – e.g. 1 pound = 500 gr., instead of 453 gr.

LIQUID MEASURES

American (Standard Cup)			Metric Equivalent
1 cup	$= \frac{1}{2}$ pint	= 8 fl. oz.	2.37 dl.
1 Tb.	$= \frac{1}{2}$ fl. oz.		1.5 cl.
1 tsp.	$= \frac{1}{6}$ fl. oz.		0.5 cl.
1 pint	= 16 fl. oz.		4.73 dl.
1 quart	= 2 pints	= 32 fl. oz.	9.46 dl.

British (Standard Cup)			Metric Equivalent
1 cup	$= \frac{1}{2}$ pint	= 10 fl. oz.	2.84 dl.
1 Tb.	= 0.55 fl. oz.		1.7 cl.
1 tsp.	$= \frac{1}{5}$ fl. oz.		0.6 cl.
1 pint	= 20 fl. oz.		5.7 dl.
1 quart	= 2 pints	= 40 fl. oz.	1.1 liter

1 cup = 16 tablespoons
1 table spoon = 3 teaspoons

1 liter = 10 deciliters = 100 centiliters

SOLID MEASURES

American/British		Metric	
1 lb.	= 16 oz.	= 453 grams	
2.2 lbs.		=1000 grams	= 1 kilogram
1 oz.		= 28 grams	
$3\frac{1}{2}$ oz.		= 100 grams	

OVEN TEMPERATURES

Regulo Gas Mark	Degrees Fahrenheit	Degrees Centigrade	
$\frac{1}{4}-\frac{1}{2}$	240–280	115–135	Very slow
1	280–320	135–160	Slow
3	320–340	160–170	Warm
4	340–370	170–185	Moderate
5–6	370–400	185–205	Fairly hot
7	400–440	205–225	Hot

For a perfect dish of pasta remember

Buy only pasta made from durum wheat.
Use a large saucepan.
Make sure that the water is boiling and salted when you drop in the pasta.
Do not overdrain pasta. It should be dripping with water.
Do not leave the kitchen while the pasta is cooking.
Taste the sauce often.
Use good ingredients for the sauce.

How much pasta to use

If you are serving pasta as the first course, 3 ounces per person is about right. For the main course this should be increased to about 4 ounces per person.

Most of the recipes in this book are for 4 people. This is stated in each case.

The quantities in the recipes are based on 3 ounces of pasta per person, and should be increased proportionately if you are serving more.

Ingredients

Herbs

The most important herbs for pasta sauces are: basil, oregano, parsley and sage. Fresh herbs are always infinitely preferable to dried ones and, although dried herbs can be substituted in some cases, the taste will be different.

Parmesan cheese

Always use fresh Italian Parmesan. It should be bought in whole pieces and grated just before use. Some Italian grocery stores sell their own freshly grated Parmesan, and this is usually quite good. Don't use packaged grated Parmesan. It is better to substitute freshly grated good Cheddar.

The pieces of Parmesan cheese should be stored in the refrigerator well wrapped in aluminium foil. If the Parmesan becomes very hard and dry, wrap it in a damp cloth for a day and then put it back in the foil in the refrigerator.

Oil

Good olive oil should be heavy and greenish in color. Do not buy olive oil which is too refined for it will not give the sauce enough taste. In some recipes, vegetable oil can be substituted for olive oil, in which case I have always noted this in the list of ingredients.

Mozzarella cheese

In America you can often find fresh mozzarella in Italian shops. Otherwise there are several commercial brands widely available.

In England, where most of the mozzarella is imported, buy the Italian variety as opposed to the Danish kind, which has a tendency to become rubbery and

tasteless when cooked. If you cannot find Italian mozzarella, Bel Paese is a very good substitute.

Tomatoes

There is no substitute for home-grown tomatoes, picked when fully ripened.

When buying tomatoes look for firm, red ones. Plum tomatoes have more flavor and are the best for sauces. Canned plum tomatoes are often better than out-of-season fresh tomatoes, which have been picked when still green and allowed to ripen in the box.

Fresh tomatoes for sauces should always be peeled and the seeds discarded. To peel them, drop each tomato into a small pan of rapidly boiling water. There should be enough water to cover the tomato easily. Leave for only a split second, then remove and peel. The skin should come off very easily. Do not leave them in for longer or they will start to cook. Cut into pieces or strips, according to the recipe, and discard the seeds.

Concentrated tomato paste is no substitute for either fresh or canned tomatoes, but it can add an extra dimension to some sauces, increase the tomato flavor and help to bind. Look for Italian brands, as they are usually sweeter.

Garlic

Garlic has played a part in many civilizations for over 2000 years. The Egyptians worshipped garlic as a god, presumably because they were familiar with its medicinal properties. In Roman times, garlic was used mostly in plebeian cooking. In the Middle Ages, Alfonso, King of Castille (1158–1214) who defeated the Moors and married the daughter of Henry II of England, so hated garlic that he punished anyone who came to court smelling of it.

Il Platina, in the first known book of European cooking, *De Honesta Voluptate ac Valetudine* (1475), recommends garlic as an antidote for dog bites. It was also reputed to steady the nerves of hysterical people, to combat epidemics and infectious diseases, and to promote the passing of urine. But perhaps its most notable and worthy function is as a deterrent against vampires. Before retiring for the night, beautiful young virgins should secure all windows and doors, place a Bible and Crucifix by their bedside, and hang at least a dozen bunches of garlic around the room. A few cloves may also be placed under the pillow and at the foot of the bed. In cases of particularly hot pursuit, three cloves of garlic should be taken after each meal; this is guaranteed to keep everybody away. Garlic is still recognized as being beneficial for the health. It purifies the blood, clears the skin and aids the digestive processes. Some Italian women eat a clove of raw garlic each day to keep their complexions clear.

Whatever its non-culinary powers, garlic has become an indispensable and central ingredient of Italian cooking. Used in moderation, and not over-cooked, it flavors sauces and enhances meat and vegetable dishes. Look for firm, fresh garlic; do not use shrivelled cloves. Garlic salt is no substitute for the real thing.

When frying garlic, do it over very gentle heat and be careful not to let it go brown because it will give a bitter taste to the sauce.

Pasta shapes

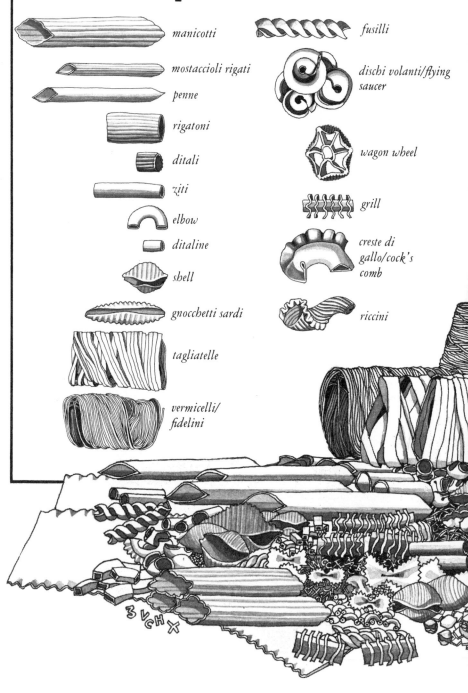

manicotti

mostaccioli rigati

penne

rigatoni

ditali

ziti

elbow

ditaline

shell

gnocchetti sardi

tagliatelle

vermicelli/
fidelini

fusilli

dischi volanti/flying
saucer

wagon wheel

grill

creste di
gallo/cock's
comb

riccini

 *ruffled lasagne*

 farfalle/noodle bow

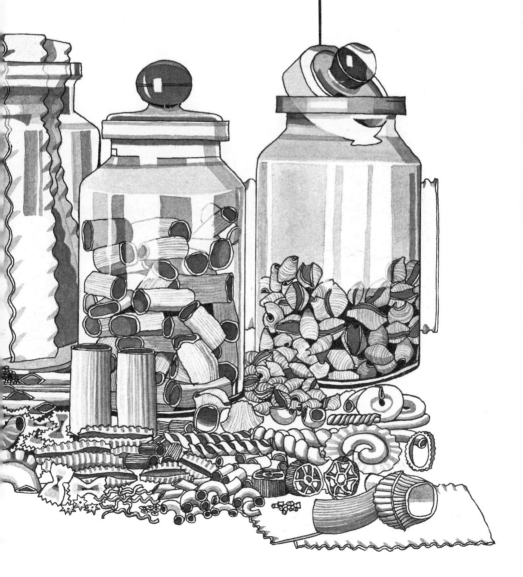

The five golden rules for cooking store-bought pasta

It is not difficult to cook pasta well, but it does require great care. *Gli spaghetti amano la compagnia* – spaghetti loves company! Never leave the kitchen while the pasta is cooking: it can't take care of itself. The timing is crucial, and just two minutes more or less can spoil a dish which in every other way is perfect. The best test to find out whether the pasta is cooked is to take some out and have a bite.

1. Use a large saucepan in which to boil the water. A wide, flat saucepan is the ideal shape, if your stove can accommodate it. The proportion of water to pasta is:

> 4 quarts to 1 pound
> 1 liter to 100 grams

2. The salt can be added to the water at the beginning, but it *must* be added at least 2 minutes before the pasta is dropped in so that it has enough time to dissolve. Add about $1\frac{1}{2}$ heaped tablespoons of salt for each pound of pasta. The quantity of salt can be increased or decreased according to the strength or saltiness of the sauce you are using.

3. The water must be boiling rapidly *before* the pasta is dropped into it. Add all the pasta at once, and stir with a wooden spoon to prevent it from sticking to itself or to the pan. If you are cooking long pasta, ease it in as rapidly as you can without breaking it. Then stir it to separate the strands. Cover the pan to bring the water back to the boil as quickly as possible, and remove the cover as soon as it does. Stir again, and then adjust heat so that the water boils fast without boiling over. Some cooks add 1 teaspoon of olive oil to the water before the pasta is added to prevent it from sticking. This is never done in Italy, and I have never found it necessary.

4. The cooking time varies according to the quality, size and shape of the pasta. If the pasta is going to be served immediately and will require no further cooking, it should be *al dente.* This means firm to the bite. To get this just right, you should try the pasta 3 or 4 minutes before the cooking instructions on the packet suggest it will be done, as the recommended time is usually excessive. The pasta is done when its "soul" (the innermost part) is still firm. Remember to drain it as soon as it reaches this point, as it will continue to cook until it is drained.

If the pasta is going to be fried, remove and drain it when it is just a little too hard, about 1 minute before it reaches the *al dente* point.

If the pasta is going to be baked (as for the pasticci recipes), remove and drain when it is still quite hard to the bite, about 5 minutes before it reaches the *al dente* point.

5. Have a colander ready in the sink. As soon as the pasta is *al dente,* pour it from the saucepan into the colander and toss it briskly 2 or 3 times. If you are using pasta with a hole, drain it a bit longer than spaghetti, but *do not over-drain any pasta.* Some Italian experts even suggest that $\frac{1}{2}$ cup of the cooking water should be reserved and added to the pasta before it is dressed if it seems too dry, and I have found this to be necessary in some of the recipes. I also recommend that a pat of butter be tossed quickly with the pasta before the sauce is added as this prevents sticking. Pasta must be eaten right away.

For the cooking of homemade pasta, see page 108.

A new method of cooking store-bought pasta

Believe it or not, there is now a new way of cooking pasta, which breaks many of the well established rules, and yet which I have found in many ways better than the traditional method. It was pioneered in Italy by Agnesi, one of the leading pasta manufacturers, and has several distinct advantages over the orthodox way of cooking pasta.

The startling thing about this method is that the pasta cooks for most of the time in water that has gone off the boil. The advantages are:

1. The pasta keeps its "soul" (the innermost part) better. Even if you leave it in the hot water for a minute or two too long, the pasta does not become gluey — as it does if left too long in boiling water.

2. Because of this, there is no need to stand over the saucepan, tasting the pasta and keeping the water on the boil. So you can do something else while the pasta is cooking; if you set the timer you don't even need to stay in the kitchen.

3. You save gas or electricity, since after boiling the water for only two minutes, you turn off the heat.

4. This method, it is claimed, allows the pasta to retain more of the natural goodness of the wheat during the cooking process. An indication of this is the fact that the water is still clear after the pasta has been cooked in it.

Try it for yourself, following these instructions:
1. Use a large saucepan containing the usual proportions of water and salt to the quantity of pasta you want to cook. When the water is boiling rapidly, put all the pasta in at once. Stir thoroughly with a wooden spoon or a long fork.
2. Cover the saucepan to bring the water back to the boil as quickly as possible. When it is boiling again, uncover the pan and boil fast for two minutes only.
3. Turn off the heat and stir thoroughly. Lay a thick kitchen cloth on the saucepan, and put the lid tightly over the cloth. Wait for the same length of time mentioned on the packet in the instructions for normal cooking.
4. Drain the pasta – but never too much. Pasta should still be dripping wet after it has been drained.

Homemade pasta

More homemade egg pasta is made in Emilia-Romagna, the provinces around Bologna, than in any other region of Italy. This is due to several factors: the cold winters which demand a higher protein diet; the exceptionally fertile land; the tradition of highly productive farming and, above all, the love the people have for good food. They would rather spend more time in making their own pasta, and be sure of its freshness, than buy the ready-made kind. Their cuisine is based on dairy products and pork, and these rich ingredients produce the ideal sauces to complement fresh egg pasta. So much importance is attributed to the ability to produce a fine *sfoglia* that when a girl from another region marries an Emilian she has to go into training with her mother-in-law before her husband will accept her.

Some Italian shops in Little Italy in New York or Soho in London sell homemade tagliatelle or ravioli, etc. which can be quite good. But I think that pasta made with eggs should be made at home.

The idea of making pasta at home may be daunting, but once you have mastered the basic technique the process takes no more than one hour from start to finish, and the result is really worth the effort. This is the traditional Emilian way of making egg pasta, and although in other regions milk, olive oil or water are sometimes added, this recipe calls only for flour and eggs. Read through all the instructions before beginning.

Ingredients

Use all-purpose (plain) flour and large eggs. It is impossible to give a hard-and-fast rule about how much flour to add to each egg because egg sizes vary, but the correct proportion is approximately $\frac{3}{4}$ cup (100 gr.) to each egg. This can be increased, but no more than 1 cup of flour per egg should be added. You will need a long thin rolling pin, at least 32 inches (80 cm.) long, and a large smooth working surface (formica is ideal).

For 3 to 4 persons
2 eggs
1½ cups (200 gr.) flour
salt

For 5 to 6 persons
3 eggs
2¼ cups (300 gr.) flour
salt

1. Place the flour in a mound on a clean working surface. Make a well in the center and break the eggs into it.   Add a pinch of salt. Start beating the eggs with a fork, gradually drawing the flour from the inside of the well. When the paste thickens, mix in the rest of the flour with your hands and quickly work it until the mixture forms a mass. It will still be lumpy. If it is too sticky and moist add a bit more flour until the mixture stops sticking to your hands.

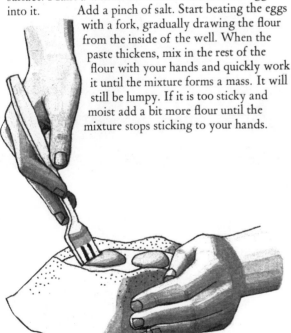

2. Set the mixture aside and thoroughly clean the working surface, using a knife to scrape off the crumbs. Then wash your hands removing every trace of dough. Dry them well.

3. Lightly flour the work surface and your hands. Knead the dough with the heel of your hands, not the palm, folding it over toward you and pressing against it away from you, one hand at a time.

Do this over and over again, turning it around as you work, for about 10 minutes or until the dough is elastic, smooth and compact.

4. If you are making the pasta with more than 2 eggs, divide the dough in half, leaving one half between two soup plates while you work on the other. Lightly flour the work surface and the rolling pin. Pat the dough into a flattish ball and begin gently rolling away from you to open the ball out. After each roll rotate the dough so that it remains circular. Repeat until the dough is about $\frac{1}{8}$ inch thick.

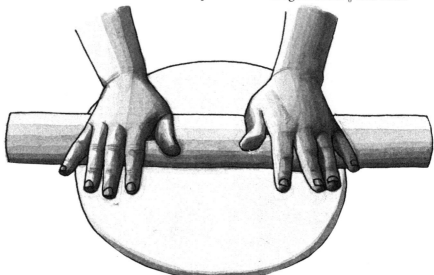

5. In order to get the pasta paper thin, a final rolling process is needed. This is slightly tricky to learn but, like riding a bicycle, once you have mastered it you will never have trouble again.

The principle is one of stretching the pasta sideways with your hands while you roll it backwards and forwards over the pin. Dust the work surface and pin lightly with flour. Curl the far end of the pasta around the middle of the rolling pin, and roll it up toward you.

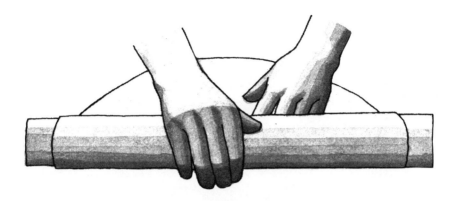

As you do this, quickly slide your hands along the pasta toward the ends of the pin, lightly stretching the pasta away from the center while you roll the pin backwards and forwards very rapidly. Then bring your hands back to the center and repeat the stretching motion as you roll up a bit more of the sheet. Continue until you have rolled up the whole of the circle of dough. While it is still wrapped around the pin, lift and turn it about 45° before unrolling the sheet. In this way you will start the thinning operation on a new piece of the sheet each time. Repeat this rolling and stretching process, making

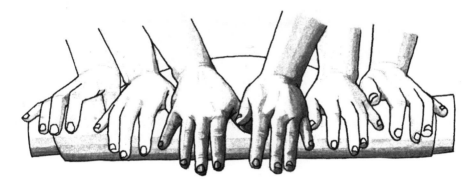

sure that the sheet is even, smooth, and has no holes or creases. If the dough is a little sticky, dust the surface again with flour. Keep rolling until the sheet becomes nearly paper thin and almost transparent, but try not to take longer than 10 minutes or the dough will become dry and lose its elasticity. This thin sheet of pasta is known as a *sfoglia.*

6. If you are making stuffed pasta (ravioli or cannelloni) the *sfoglia* must not be allowed to dry (see pages 186, 183). If you are making any other kind of pasta (*fettuccine,* tagliatelle, lasagne, etc.) place a clean, dry towel on a table and lay the *sfoglia* on it to dry, letting about one-third of the sheet hang over the edge of the table. Turn every 10 minutes. The drying should take about 30 minutes, depending on the room temperature. The pasta is ready to cut when it is dry to the touch and begins to look leathery. Make sure that it does not get too dry or it will be impossible to fold and cut.

7. Bring the *sfoglia* to a cutting board. The easiest way to carry it is to roll it back onto the rolling pin.

For *tagliolini,* tagliatelle and *fettuccine:*
Fold the *sfoglia* into a flat roll, approximately 3 inches wide. Cut the pasta into the width desired. Gently unfold the rolls of noodles and let them dry for at least 10 minutes.

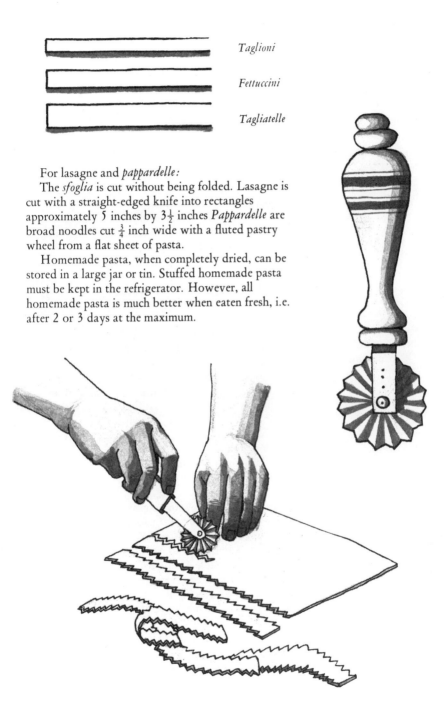

Taglioni

Fettuccini

Tagliatelle

For lasagne and *pappardelle:*

The *sfoglia* is cut without being folded. Lasagne is cut with a straight-edged knife into rectangles approximately 5 inches by $3\frac{1}{2}$ inches *Pappardelle* are broad noodles cut $\frac{3}{4}$ inch wide with a fluted pastry wheel from a flat sheet of pasta.

Homemade pasta, when completely dried, can be stored in a large jar or tin. Stuffed homemade pasta must be kept in the refrigerator. However, all homemade pasta is much better when eaten fresh, i.e. after 2 or 3 days at the maximum.

Pasta machine.
Vera Collingwood

Sfoglia (homemade pasta
sheets) made with the
pasta machine

Cooking homemade pasta

Homemade pasta cooks in very little time, so have
everything ready for serving or further cooking before
you drop the pasta into the boiling water.

For 1 pound (500 gr.) of pasta, boil at least 4 quarts
(4 liters) of water in a very large saucepan. Add $1\frac{1}{2}$
heaped tablespoons of salt for each pound of pasta.

When the water is boiling very rapidly, drop in all
the pasta at once (for lasagne or cannelloni see
individual recipes). It will sink to the bottom. Quickly
bring the water back to the boil. The cooking time
varies according to the size and thickness of the pasta,
and pasta for stuffing always takes longer, but once the
water returns to the boil the pasta will be done very
quickly. Cooking time varies from about 2 to 5
minutes, so start tasting after about 1 minute. The rule,
as for dry pasta, is to taste homemade pasta of any kind
soon after the water returns to the boil.

It has been proved that the best homemade pasta is
the result of hand kneading and "elbow grease."
However, most people nowadays cannot afford to
spend as much time in the kitchen as their grandmothers
did, and the pasta machine helps to produce those
homemade results in much less time and with very little
loss of quality. Remember that when you use the
machine the dough must be drier, and you may have to
add more flour.

Make your dough following steps 1 and 2 of the
homemade pasta recipe on page 102.

3. Knead the dough with your hands for 3 to 4
minutes to begin the amalgamation. Divide the mass
into balls the size of oranges. Work on one ball at a
time, leaving the others to rest between two soup plates.
Adjust the smooth kneading rollers at one end of the
machine to their widest setting, and pass the ball
through 5 or 6 times, folding it over and turning it after
each kneading. Do not fold it the last time. If it sticks
add a bit more flour. Adjust the rollers to the next
thinnest setting, and pass the *sfoglia* through once.
Repeat for each remaining roller setting, passing the
unfolded sheet once through each of them. If the *sfoglia*
gets too long (over 2 feet or 60 cm.) cut it in half and
proceed with one half at a time; otherwise it will break

and clog the machine. After it has been through all the
settings you should have an even, smooth and uniform
strip of pasta. Leave it between two clean cloths while
you repeat the process with the remaining balls.
4. If you are making stuffed pasta, proceed
immediately with the desired recipe.

For *tagliolini*: pass the *sfoglia* through the narrowest
cutting blades, separate, and leave to dry for 10 to 15
minutes.

For tagliatelle: pass the *sfoglia* through the broad
cutting blades, separate, and leave to dry for 10 to 15
minutes.

Some egg pasta is green. This is because a small
quantity of spinach has been added to the dough. The
primary purpose of the spinach is to color the dough
and, although the taste is not affected very much, it
helps to make the pasta creamier and softer. Cooking
time for spinach pasta is slightly longer. This green
sfoglia is usually used for tagliatelle, or lasagne.

Spinach pasta
Pasta verde

8 ounces (250 gr.) fresh spinach or 5 ounces (160 gr.)
*   frozen spinach, chopped*
2 eggs
2 to 2½ cups all-purpose (plain) flour
salt

1. If you are using fresh spinach, pick it over very
carefully discarding the stems and any discolored or
limp leaves. Fill a sink or a large bowl with cold water
and plunge the spinach into it. Wash it well, changing
the water until there is no more sand at the bottom.
Cook the spinach in a covered saucepan, with a little
salt, over moderately high heat for about 10 minutes.
Stir occasionally to prevent it from sticking and
burning. Drain and cool. Squeeze it between your
hands to remove all liquid, and dry it in a clean cloth.
Chop very finely.
2. If you are using frozen spinach, follow the cooking
instructions on the package. Drain it and allow to cool.
Dry the spinach in a clean cloth.
3. Proceed with the instructions for homemade pasta
(page 102) adding the chopped spinach with the eggs.

Spinach pasta can also be made with the pasta
machine (see above). In this case it will need more flour
to prevent the *sfoglia* from sticking and clogging the
machine.

Basic sauces

All these sauces can be used by themselves or as a base for more elaborate dishes. They can all be made in advance, and kept in the refrigerator for up to 4 to 5 days or frozen. The two meat sauces (*ragú*) are perfect dressings for short or homemade pasta, while the tomato sauces which follow are better for spaghetti, *fidelini* or any long pasta. All the 5 sauces are for dressing 12 ounces (350 gr.) of pasta, 4 first course helpings.

Ragú **Bolognese**
Ragú bolognese

This is the classic sauce used in Bologna for baked lasagne.

> *8 ounces (250 gr.) ground chuck steak, with all fat removed*
> *2 ounces (30 gr.) chicken livers, chopped and with any greenish and fatty spots removed*
> *2 slices streaky bacon, unsmoked, or **pancetta***
> *1 tablespoon (15 gr.) butter*
> *2 tablespoons (30 gr.) dripping or good lard*
> *1 onion, finely chopped*
> *1 small carrot, finely chopped*
> *1 celery stick, finely chopped*
> *1 clove garlic, finely chopped*
> *1 bay leaf*
> *½ cup red wine*
> *1½ tablespoons tomato paste*
> *½ cup of stock*
> *pinch of nutmeg*
> *salt and freshly ground black pepper*

1. In a saucepan, combine the bacon with the butter and dripping, and cook gently. After about 1 minute add the onion, and when it begins to soften (after approximately 5 minutes), add the celery, carrot and garlic. Stir well; add the bay leaf, chicken livers and the tomato paste, and cook gently for 4 to 5 minutes.
2. Add the beef, raise the heat and cook rapidly until the meat barely ceases to look raw. Stir properly to break up the clumps of meat. Add the wine, and cook over high heat until it has almost all evaporated (approximately 2 to 3 minutes).
3. Add the stock, mix well, adjust seasoning and add the nutmeg. Cover and simmer over very low heat for about 1½ hours. If the sauce gets too dry add a little

warm water. Remove the bay leaf before using the sauce.

Variations:

You can use half ground beef and half ground pork, or half beef and half sausages, skinned and mashed. These should be the Italian variety, mild, thick-grained, and without herbs. For a more delicate sauce, add $\frac{1}{2}$ cup light (single) cream, and then warm the sauce for 1 minute before using it. For a stronger sauce, substitute $\frac{1}{2}$ a small dry hot red pepper, crumbled, for the black pepper.

This is a chunkier *ragú*, made with cubed, rather than ground steak.

Old-fashioned *ragú*
Ragú all'antica

8 ounces (250 gr.) chuck steak, in one piece
1 pound (500 gr.) fresh tomatoes, peeled, or canned plum
    tomatoes, put through the food mill
4 tablespoons (60 gr.) butter
1 small onion, chopped
$\frac{1}{2}$ cup red wine
$\frac{1}{2}$ tablespoon all-purpose (plain) flour
2 tablespoons heavy (double) cream
1 clove
salt and freshly ground black pepper

1. Melt 3 tablespoons (45 gr.) of the butter in a saucepan, and sauté the onion for about 5 minutes. Add the meat, and brown on all sides over medium heat. Cook for about 10 minutes.
2. Lift the meat from the saucepan, transfer it to a wooden board, and chop it into small pieces. Return it to the pan and cook for a further 5 minutes. Add the flour and mix rapidly to brown for 1 minute. Add the tomatoes, remaining butter, salt, pepper and the clove. Bring the sauce back to the boil, and cook over high heat for a few minutes.
3. Lower the heat, cover, and simmer gently for about 1 hour. Turn off the heat, and remove the clove. Stir in the cream and warm the sauce for 1 minute before using it.

This is a recipe for a simple tomato sauce. It can be used on its own or as a base for sauces which involve more ingredients. This sauce keeps very well in the refrigerator for a few days.

Plain tomato sauce
Sugo di pomodoro

1 pound (500 gr.) fresh tomatoes, peeled and quartered, or
*   canned plum tomatoes*
1 onion, quartered
1 small stick of celery, cut into pieces
1 clove garlic
1 bay leaf
4 to 5 leaves of fresh basil or a sprig of parsley
1 teaspoon sugar

1. Put all ingredients in a small saucepan and boil over moderate heat, uncovered, until the onion is soft, approximately 20 to 30 minutes, stirring every now and then to prevent sticking. If you are using fresh tomatoes, add $\frac{1}{2}$ cup of water.
2. Remove the bay leaf and the garlic, and pass through a food mill. If you wish to use the sauce at once, simply reheat gently and pour it over freshly cooked pasta which has already been tossed with olive oil or butter.

Neapolitan tomato sauce
Sugo di pomodoro alla
napoletana

1 pound (500 gr.) fresh tomatoes, peeled or canned plum
*   tomatoes*
1 clove garlic, chopped or crushed
a small bunch of fresh basil leaves, roughly torn, or chopped
*   fresh parsley or dried oregano*
5 tablespoons olive oil
salt and freshly ground black pepper
1 teaspoon sugar

1. Combine the tomatoes (if you are using fresh tomatoes add 2 tablespoons of water), olive oil, garlic, basil, sugar, salt and pepper in a small saucepan and boil over moderate high heat, uncovered, for about 10 minutes or until the oil has separated from the tomatoes.

Emilian tomato sauce
Sugo di pomodoro
all'emiliana

While the Neapolitan sauce is particularly good for spaghetti, this Emilian sauce is better with homemade pasta or short pasta, like macaroni or *penne*.

1 pound (500 gr.) fresh peeled tomatoes or canned plum
*   tomatoes*
1 small onion, chopped
1 celery stick, chopped
1 clove garlic
1 tablespoon tomato paste
6 tablespoons (90 gr.) butter
$\frac{1}{4}$ cup red wine

fresh basil or parsley
salt and freshly ground black pepper
1 teaspoon sugar

1. In a small saucepan combine 4 tablespoons (60 gr.) of the butter with the onion, celery and garlic and sauté them, pressing against the pan to release the juices, until soft (approximately 10 minutes).
2. Add the tomatoes (if you use canned tomatoes discard some of the juice), the tomato paste, the sugar and the wine and boil rapidly for 15 to 20 minutes, stirring every now and then.
3. Purée the sauce through a food mill and add a few torn leaves of basil or a bunch of chopped parsley.

Béchamel sauce

Béchamel is a simple sauce and can be made very quickly. Like some other sauces which were supposedly "discovered" in the seventeenth century by the French, Béchamel was already known in Italy. It was a sauce called *Balsamella*, made from milk, flour and butter, and it was a vital ingredient of many pasta dishes, especially those made with lasagne.

For 2 cups of medium Béchamel
2½ cups milk
4 tablespoons (60 gr.) butter
6 tablespoons (50 to 60 gr.) all-purpose (plain) flour
salt and freshly ground black pepper
   For a thicker sauce, increase the quantities of butter and flour, but make sure that you always use slightly more butter than flour to prevent lumps.

1. In a small saucepan slowly bring the milk to simmering point.
2. Meanwhile, melt the butter over very low heat in a heavy-bottomed saucepan.
3. When the butter is melted, add the flour, and stir well with a wooden spoon. Cook for 1 minute, stirring constantly, until the mixture is golden, but not brown. Remove from the heat and add the hot milk, a few tablespoons at a time, stirring constantly until all the milk has been incorporated and the sauce is smooth.
4. Add salt and pepper. Return the saucepan to the heat, and slowly bring the sauce to the boil, stirring constantly. Boil for 2 to 3 minutes for a medium sauce, or 6 to 7 minutes for a thicker sauce. If the sauce is lumpy, pass it through a strainer before using.

If you do not wish to use the sauce immediately, float a thin film of milk or melted butter on top to prevent a skin from forming. Set aside uncovered. Keep it warm by standing the pan over a pilot light, or refrigerate. It will keep for 2 to 3 days.

Flavorings:

1. Nutmeg is the most common flavoring, and a pinch can be added with the salt and pepper.
2. For a garlic-flavored sauce, add 1 clove of garlic to the milk when it is being heated, and remove before adding the milk to the butter and flour mixture. No nutmeg is used in this case.
3. For an onion-flavored sauce, sauté, very gently, half of a grated onion in the butter. When cooked (approximately 3 minutes), add the flour and proceed from step 3.

Uncooked tomato sauces for spaghetti

These sauces are very easy to make, and since they are not cooked, the ingredients must be particularly tasty and fresh. Choose well-ripened tomatoes, fresh herbs and good quality olive oil. Many variations on these are possible, and it is easy and fun to create new tastes by substituting seasonings or adding different ingredients to the basic mixture.

Spaghetti with uncooked sauce I

For 4 persons
12 ounces (350 gr.) spaghetti
12 ounces (350 gr.) fresh tomatoes
5 tablespoons olive oil
1 clove garlic, finely chopped or whole
10 to 12 fresh basil leaves, torn into 2 or 3 pieces each, or
    2 tablespoons fresh parsley, finely chopped
salt and freshly ground black pepper

1. Peel the tomatoes one at a time. To do this, drop each tomato into a small pan of rapidly boiling water. There should be enough water to cover the tomato easily. Leave for only a split second, then remove and peel. The skin should come off very easily. Do not leave them in for longer or they will start to cook. Cut into pieces and discard the seeds. Chop very coarsely.

2. Place the tomato pieces in a shallow bowl with the other ingredients. Stir well. Leave to marinate for at least 6 hours. If you are using a whole clove of garlic, remove it before serving.

3. When the sauce is ready, cook and drain the spaghetti. Turn it into a very hot dish, cover with the uncooked sauce, and serve immediately.

Variation:

Combine all the ingredients except the olive oil and the spaghetti in the blender. Blend to a smooth sauce. When the pasta is cooked, toss it first with the oil and then with the sauce, which needs no marinating.

Spaghetti with uncooked sauce II

For 4 persons
12 ounces (350 gr.) spaghetti
12 ounces (350 gr.) fresh tomatoes, peeled
½ Spanish onion, coarsely chopped
5 tablespoons olive oil
oregano
salt and freshly ground black pepper

1. Prepare the tomatoes as in the preceding recipe.
2. Combine all the ingredients except the spaghetti in a bowl and leave to marinate for at least 6 hours. Proceed as for recipe I.

Spaghetti with uncooked sauce III

For 4 persons
12 ounces (350 gr.) spaghetti
12 ounces (350 gr.) fresh tomatoes, peeled
5 tablespoons olive oil
2 cloves garlic
1 tablespoon chopped parsley
4 ounces (125 gr.) green olives, stoned and coarsely chopped
1 small dried hot red pepper, broken into 2 or 3 pieces
1 tablespoon capers
salt and freshly ground black pepper

1. Proceed as for recipe I, adding the capers, olives, and hot red pepper pieces to the marinade. The garlic may be chopped or left whole. Let stand for at least 6 hours.
2. Just before serving, remove the red pepper pieces and the cloves of garlic if you have used them whole.

Recipes from the past

Many people are fascinated with the past. Part of the fascination lies in the wondering what life was really like, what the people were really like. We should love to project ourselves backwards in time to get a real feel of everyday life as it used to be. One of the only ways to do this is to cook with ancient recipes, and eat exactly what people ate hundreds of years ago. For a few minutes you can be a Renaissance man, or woman, and know exactly the tastes that they knew.

You may find some of the ingredients difficult to get nowadays: try asking for goat's milk or the meat of a young heifer, at your local supermarket! Where this applies I have substituted modern equivalents. Many of these recipes suggest cooking pasta in various broths. I diligently tried this way, but cannot detect any difference from the usual method of cooking it in water.

Until the eighteenth century, pasta was usually dressed with sauces that were both sweet and spicy and even the savory recipes called for a certain amount of sugar.

Horace's chickpea,
laganelle **and leek soup**
La minestra di Orazio

In ancient Rome pasta made with durum flour and water was baked on hot, porous, large stones. It was then cut into strips and used in soup. Sometimes it was fried instead of baked.

This recipe is my adaptation of the famous dish referred to by Horace in one of his satires, "*Ad porri et ciceris refero, laganique catinum*" ("I am going home to a bowl of leeks and chickpeas and lasagne"). It is one of the earliest references to any kind of pasta.

For 6 persons
6 ounces (190 gr.) **laganelle** *or squares*
6 ounces (190 gr.) dried chickpeas
6 cups water
1 leek
1 celery stalk, chopped
1 bay leaf, crushed
3 or 4 fresh tomatoes, peeled, seeded and roughly chopped
½ cup olive oil
parsley, chopped
salt and pepper

1. Soak the chickpeas overnight in warm water, changing the water once. Drain them and rinse them with fresh water.
2. Put the chickpeas into a large saucepan. Add the water, the white part of the leek cut into small rings, the tomatoes, celery, bay leaf, salt and a good quantity of freshly ground pepper. Cover tightly, and bring the soup rapidly to the boil. Lower the heat and simmer for about 3 hours. Do not uncover the pan or the chickpeas will become hard and will not cook through.
3. Part boil the pasta in a separate saucepan full of boiling water. Drain and fry it in the olive oil. Add the pasta and the oil to the soup, and cook until the pasta is tender. Add the parsley. A bowl of freshly grated Parmesan can be served on the side, if desired.

The first pasta recipe as such appears in a fourteenth-century cook book.

Common ravioli with
leaves
Rafioli comun de herbe
vantazati

"If you want to make ravioli with leaves, pick some leaves, clean them well and wash them. Boil them a little, take them out and squeeze them well and cut them with the knife and then pound them in the mortar. And take some fresh cheese and some sour cheese and eggs and sweet and spicy spices and sultanas and mix

well together and make a paste. And then make a thin
sfoglia and take little pieces of the mixture and make the
ravioli. When they are made, cook them, and when
they are cooked powder them on top with an abundant
quantity of spices and with good cheese and butter.
And they are very good."

This is a modern version of this recipe for 4 to 5
persons.

*Ravioli made with 2¼ cups (200 gr.) all-purpose
(plain) flour (see page 102)*
*1 pound (500 gr.) fresh spinach or beet leaves or 10 ounces
(300 gr.) frozen spinach*
4 ounces (125 gr.) cottage cheese
½ cup (50 gr.) Parmesan cheese or good Cheddar, grated
1 egg
6 tablespoons (90 gr.) butter
¼ cup (45 gr.) raisins (sultanas)
salt
1 teaspoon cinnamon
½ teaspoon nutmeg

1. If you are using fresh spinach, pick it over carefully
discarding the stems and any discolored or limp leaves.
Fill a sink or a large bowl with cold water and plunge
the spinach into it. Wash it well, changing the water
until there is no more sand at the bottom. Cook the
spinach in a covered pan with a little salt, over
moderately high heat for about 10 minutes. Stir
occasionally. Drain and cool. Squeeze it between your
hands to remove all liquid. Chop very finely.
2. In a mixing bowl, combine all the ingredients and
mix very thoroughly.
3. Make the ravioli (see page 186) using the spinach
stuffing.
4. Drop the ravioli into a large saucepan of salted,
boiling water. They are cooked when they come to the
surface (approximately 5 minutes). Lift them very
gently from the saucepan and put them into a warm
serving dish. Toss them with the butter, which should
be melted previously, and serve them with a bowl of
grated Parmesan on the side.

From the same book comes also the following recipe
for lasagne (this may be the origin of what we now
know as stuffed cannelloni).
"If you want to make lasagne for Lent, take the

*Eighteenth-century
colander for pasta
used in central Italy.*
Vera Collingwood

lasagne and cook them and take some walnuts, cleaned and well pounded, and put them inside the lasagne. And when you take them to the table, serve them and sprinkle them with spices and sugar."

A recipe from the book *Libro de Arte Coquinaria* by Mastro Martino, mid-fifteenth century, for vermicelli: "Take some flour, which must be of the best quality, add water and spin it thin, cutting it into small pieces with the fingers and put it to dry in the sun, and it will keep for two and even three years. And when you will want to cook it, do so in a meat broth or in a broth of a beautiful fat chicken for one hour. And then put on it grated cheese and spices. If it is fasting time, cook it in almond milk and sugar or in goat milk. And because this milk does not like to boil as long as the vermicelli, boil the vermicelli first with a little water, as you would for rice. And in a similar way you must cook *tritte* or *fermentine* [minced pasta, probably so called because it resembles a grain of corn, *frumento*]."

The next two recipes are also of historical, rather than practical, interest. They are from *De Honesta Voluptate ac Valetudine* published in 1475, and written in Latin by Bartolomeo Sacchi, famous as Il Platina. This was by far the best known cookbook of the Renaissance period, and it went to nine editions between 1475 and 1500.

A food called vermicelli
Vivanda dicta vermicelli

"Flour, well-sieved and white, well-kneaded with water, rolled into thin sheets and cut in pieces the length and the width of a finger. If well dried in the sun, it will keep for 2 or 3 years. Cook them in a fatty broth and in a dish prepare them with fresh cheese and sweet spices. This pasta needs two hours of cooking."

Roman lasagne
Esicium romanicum

"The flour should be well sifted, mixed with water and prepared extended on a table. It should be rolled with an oblong polished piece of wood such as bakers use for this purpose. Then it should be drawn out and cut up to the length of a little finger, or a ribbon. It should be cooked in a fatty broth, kept on the boil. During fasting time, it should be cooked with butter and salt. When cooked, it should be transferred to a vessel and served with cheese, butter, sugar and aromatic sweet spices."

Cristoforo da Messisbugo lived in Ferrara in the sixteenth century and became steward to the Duke of

Este. His book *Libro nuovo nel qual s'insegna il modo d'ordinar banchetti* (*A New Book on How to Give Banquets*) tells how the courses should be ordered and what type of entertainment should accompany the banquet. This ranged from literary discussions to dancing. A Sunday dinner during Carnival given by two gentlemen of Ferrara for Don Ercole d'Este, included among its "fourth courses" (puddings) a plate of "*Maccheroni Napolitaine*." The dish consisted of "royal pastry, fried with honey and sugar on top." The pasta was made with durum flour and water, rolled out very thinly and cut into strips. Each strip was then rolled around a reed or a knitting needle.

The following rough translation of this recipe gives us an idea of this Renaissance pudding.

"Cook the macaroni very slowly in milk and butter. The pasta must absorb nearly all the liquid while cooking. Before it is completely cooked, remove a few spoonfuls of the milk and mix it with honey and a little ricotta. Pour this sweet sauce over the pasta and sprinkle liberally with cinnamon."

Messisbugo was less precise than Platina in his cooking time: he directed that macaroni should be cooked for the same time it takes to recite a 'Miserere'!

This is another recipe created by Cristoforo da Messisbugo for his master, the Duke of Ferrara. Yet again the ingredients are local, as so often in Italian cooking. Fish from the Adriatic sea, very near Ferrara, are excellent, especially the sole, which have quite a unique and delicate flavor.

Timpano of lasagne with fillets of sole and shrimp
Timpano di lasagne al Duca d'Este

For 4 persons
Homemade pasta made with 3 eggs and 2¼ cups all-purpose (plain) flour (see page 102)
1 pound (500 gr.) shrimp
4 sole, filleted
16 tablespoons (250 gr.) butter
1 cup (100 gr.) Parmesan cheese, freshly grated
3 tablespoons (25 to 30 gr.) all-purpose (plain) flour
1¼ cups dry white wine
2 to 3 bay leaves
4 to 5 peppercorns
1 cup water
1 onion
2 tablespoons brandy
salt and freshly ground black pepper

1. Boil the shrimp in the water and 1 cup of the wine, together with the onion, bay leaves and peppercorns, for about 15 minutes. Drain, reserving the strained liquid.

2. Gently fry the fillets of sole in 8 tablespoons (125 gr.) of the butter for 5 minutes, taking great care not to break them. Pour over the remaining wine and cook, over very low heat, for a further 5 to 7 minutes. Add salt and keep warm.

3. Shell the shrimp and sauté them in 6 tablespoons (90 gr.) of the butter for 5 minutes. Pour over the brandy and set alight. Keep warm.

4. In a small heavy-bottomed saucepan melt the remaining butter, add the flour and mix rapidly, with a wooden spoon, over very low heat. Remove from heat and gradually stir in the liquid in which the shrimp have boiled. Return the saucepan to the heat and bring the sauce to the boil, stirring constantly. Adjust seasoning. Simmer for 10 minutes, and continue to stir. Remove from heat and add the grated Parmesan. Keep warm.

5. Preheat the oven to 350°F (Gas Mark 4).

6. Cut and cook the lasagne (see recipe for "Stuffed cannelloni" on page 183).

7. Cover a buttered shallow oven dish with a layer of lasagne, spread half of the shrimp, cover again with lasagne and then with the sole. Repeat these four layers, pouring over also the juices of the two fish, and finish with the lasagne. Cover with the fish sauce, dot with a little extra butter and bake in the oven until golden (approximately ½ hour).

Spaghetti with almonds, ricotta and sweet spices
Spaghetti con salsa rinascimentale

A Renaissance recipe by Cristoforo da Messisbugo, steward to the Duke d'Este of Ferrara. The Estes were great patrons of the arts and great lovers of good living. As recorded in Messisbugo's book, their lavish banquets were unrivalled in the whole of Europe for their sumptuousness. This pasta sauce is, however, very simple to make and it has a very unusual and subtle taste.

For 4 persons
12 ounces (350 gr.) spaghetti
1 cup (100 gr.) almonds, blanched and peeled*
4 ounces (125 gr.) ricotta or cottage cheese

* When you buy almonds, make sure they are not stale. Stale almonds have a very bitter and unpleasant taste, and even the smallest quantity can ruin an otherwise delicious dish.

$\frac{1}{4}$ cup (25 gr.) Parmesan cheese, freshly grated
a good pinch of nutmeg
$\frac{1}{2}$ teaspoon cinnamon
$\frac{1}{2}$ cup light (single) cream
3 tablespoons olive oil
4 tablespoons (60 gr.) butter
salt

1. Pound the almonds in a mortar with the ricotta,
cinnamon, nutmeg, cream and oil, and reduce to a thick
paste. Add the grated Parmesan, the salt, and mix
thoroughly with a wooden spoon.
2. Cook the spaghetti. Drain, reserving $\frac{1}{2}$ cup of the
water in which it has cooked, turn it into a warm
serving dish, and dress with the butter.
3. Add the water to the sauce. Pour the sauce over the
spaghetti, and serve at once.

This dish was served as an entrée at the court of the
Duke of Montefeltro in his palace in Urbino. Federico
da Montefeltro was perhaps the greatest of all
Renaissance men: a great soldier, statesman, humanist,
man of letters and patron of the arts. His palace stands
witness to his artistic taste, and this dish proves that he
was also a connoisseur of gastronomic delights.

Timballo of lasagne with ham and cheeses
Timballo di lasagne alla Montefeltro

For 6 persons
*Homemade pasta made with 4 eggs and 3 cups (400 gr.)
    all-purpose (plain) flour (see page 102)*
2 ounces (60 gr.) mozzarella, diced
2 ounces (60 gr.) Bel Paese, diced
4 ounces (125 gr.) ham or tongue, cut into thin strips
1 cup (100 gr.) Parmesan cheese, freshly grated
*Béchamel sauce made with 2$\frac{1}{2}$ cups milk (see page 113)
    and flavored with a good pinch of nutmeg*
$\frac{1}{2}$ cup heavy (double) cream
6 tablespoons (90 gr.) butter
salt and freshly ground black pepper

1. Cut and cook the lasagne (see recipe for "Stuffed
cannelloni" on page 183).
2. Combine together the diced cheeses and the ham
with the cream. Adjust seasoning.
3. Preheat the oven to 350°F (Gas Mark 4).
4. Butter a deep oven dish and fill it with alternate
layers of lasagne and the cheese and ham mixture. Dot
each layer of lasagne with the butter and sprinkle with

the grated Parmesan. Finish with a layer of lasagne, cover with the Béchamel and bake until golden brown (approximately $\frac{1}{2}$ hour). If necessary put under the broiler (grill) for a few minutes.

***Timpano* of lasagne, prosciutto and mozzarella**
Timpano di lasagne di Bartolomeo Scappi

A sixteenth-century recipe by Bartolomeo Scappi, chef to Pope Pius V. This is a most delicate and delicious dish, but rather expensive, because of the truffle. You can omit the truffle, but the taste would certainly not be the same. The original recipe requires "the meat of a young heifer," for which I substituted veal.

For 4 persons
Homemade pasta made with 3 eggs and 2¼ cups (300 gr.) all-purpose (plain) flour (see page 102)
8 ounces (250 gr.) prosciutto (raw ham)
3 ounces (90 gr.) mozzarella or scamorza or provolone, diced
1 cup (100 gr.) Parmesan cheese, freshly grated
2 eggs
6 tablespoons (90 gr.) butter
½ cup heavy (double) cream
1 pound (500 gr.) boneless roast of veal
½ cup dry white wine
½ cup chicken stock or bouillon
pinch of nutmeg
salt and freshly ground black pepper
1 white truffle, grated

1. In a saucepan into which the veal will just fit, brown the meat on all sides in 4 tablespoons (60 gr.) of the butter. Pour over the wine, raise the heat, and reduce the liquid by half. Add the stock, adjust seasoning and simmer, covered, for about 1 hour. If necessary, add a few tablespoons of warm water during the cooking.
2. Remove the meat (you can serve it cold the next day). Scrape the bottom of the saucepan with a metal spoon and add enough cold water to obtain approximately $\frac{1}{2}$ cup of juice. Return the saucepan to the heat and boil rapidly for 1 minute, stirring constantly. Keep warm.
3. Beat the eggs and cream together and add half of the Parmesan. Beat again until a paste is formed. Add the nutmeg.
4. Preheat the oven to 350°F (Gas Mark 4).

5. Line a buttered oven dish with long thin slices of prosciutto, slightly overlapping.

6. Cut and cook the lasagne (see recipe for "Stuffed Cannelloni" on page 183). Lay some lasagne over the prosciutto, pour over some of the egg mixture and the roast juices. Cover with some mozzarella and sprinkle with the truffle. Repeat these layers until all ingredients are used up, finishing with the egg mixture. Top with the remaining Parmesan and dot with the remaining butter. Bake in the oven for approximately 20 minutes or until the top is golden.

This dish is supposed to have been created by Cardinal Alberoni of Piacenza in the eighteenth century, who was equally distinguished as soldier, churchman and, judging by this recipe, gourmet.

Timpano* of macaroni with shrimp and mushrooms
Timpano del Cardinal Alberoni

For 4 persons
12 ounces (350 gr.) noodle bows
6 ounces (180 gr.) shrimp (prawns), shelled
5 ounces (150 gr.) mushrooms, very finely sliced
1 cup (100 gr.) Parmesan cheese, freshly grated
8 tablespoons (125 gr.) butter
2 tablespoons brandy
Béchamel sauce made with 1¼ cups milk, 2 tablespoons (30 gr.) butter and 2½ tablespoons (30 gr.) all-purpose (plain) flour, flavored with a good pinch of nutmeg
salt and freshly ground black pepper

1. Sauté the mushrooms in 4 tablespoons (60 gr.) of the butter for 5 minutes.
2. Drop the pasta into rapidly boiling salted water.
3. Sauté the shrimp in 4 tablespoons (60 gr.) of the butter for 5 minutes, pour over the brandy, and set alight. Add half of the grated Parmesan and mix thoroughly. Keep warm.
4. Preheat the oven to 350°F (Gas Mark 4).
5. Drain the pasta when very *al dente*. Butter a deep oven dish and fill it with alternate layers of pasta, mushrooms and shrimp (with the juice from the cooking), in this order, finishing with the pasta.
6. Melt the remaining butter in a small saucepan, and, when the foam has subsided, pour it over the pasticcio. Top with the Béchamel, and sprinkle with the remaining cheese. Bake in the oven for approximately ½ hour. The top should be golden.

Timpano of macaroni with capon breast and prosciutto
Timpano di maccheroni alla Pompadour

An eighteenth-century Neapolitan recipe by the Prince of Francavilla. There are quite a few recipes created by this nobleman. He used to dictate them to his secretary, Don Vincenzo Corrado, who was also a great gourmet. I have been unable to find out why this *timpano* is dedicated to Madame de Pompadour.

The pasticcio is very good without the truffle. If you can afford the truffle, however, a delicious dish becomes one that is out of this world.

For 4 to 5 persons
12 ounces (350 gr.) **penne** *or rigatoni*
1 pound (500 gr.) boneless pork loin
½ cup dry white wine
½ cup chicken stock or bouillon
1 cup (200 gr.) cooked capon breast, cut into thin strips
3 ounces (90 gr.) prosciutto (raw ham), cut into Julienne strips
1 cup (100 gr.) Parmesan cheese, freshly grated
3 egg yolks
½ cup heavy (double) cream
6 tablespoons (90 gr.) butter
pinch of nutmeg
a sprig of rosemary
salt and freshly ground black pepper
1 small white or black truffle, grated (optional)

1. In a saucepan into which the pork will just fit, brown the meat on all sides in the butter. Pour over the wine, raise the heat, and reduce the liquid by half. Add the rosemary and the stock, adjust the seasoning, and simmer, covered, for about 1 hour. If necessary, add a few tablespoons of warm water during the cooking.
2. Remove the meat (you can use it cold the next day) and the rosemary. Scrape the bottom of the saucepan with a metal spoon and add enough cold water to obtain approximately ½ cup of juice. Return the saucepan to the heat and boil rapidly for 1 to 2 minutes, stirring constantly. Keep warm.
3. Preheat the oven to 350°F (Gas Mark 4).
4. Drop the pasta into rapidly boiling salted water.
5. In a bowl combine the egg yolks with the cream, cheese, nutmeg and the truffle. Mix thoroughly.
6. Drain the pasta when very *al dente*. Return it to the pot and dress it with the roast juices.
7. Butter a deep oven dish and fill it with alternate layers of pasta, capon and prosciutto, finishing with a

layer of pasta. Cover with the egg mixture, and bake until the topping becomes thick and practically solid (approximately 20 minutes). Leave the pasticcio to rest for 5 to 10 minutes before serving.

This is another eighteenth-century recipe which comes from the book of recipes by Don Vincenzo Corrado, secretary to the Prince of Francavilla.

Boiled vermicelli with sweet-and-sour tomato sauce
Vermicelli al sugo del settecento

For 4 persons
12 ounces (350 gr.) thin spaghetti
a plain tomato sauce made with 2 pounds (1000 gr.) of tomatoes (see page 111)
½ cup olive oil
2 cloves
1 hot red chili pepper, crumbled
1 teaspoon sugar
½ teaspoon cinnamon, or more, according to taste
1 cup (100 gr.) Parmesan cheese, freshly grated

1. At least 1 hour before using it, add to the sauce all the other ingredients except the Parmesan and the spaghetti. This gives time for the sauce to absorb their flavors.
2. Drop the spaghetti into rapidly boiling salted water.
3. Warm the sauce over very low heat.
4. Drain the pasta, sprinkle with half of the grated Parmesan, and dress with the sauce. Mix thoroughly and serve at once, with the remaining Parmesan on the side.

This is another eighteenth-century recipe from Naples passed on to me by my Neapolitan grandfather, who wanted to perpetuate the art of traditional Neapolitan cooking.
It is an easy and excellent dish, but it demands the finest ingredients: the best tomatoes and the best olive oil (see page 96).

Baked vermicelli with tomatoes
Torta settecentesca di vermicelli e pomodori

For 4 persons
8 ounces (250 gr.) vermicelli or thin spaghetti
1¼ pounds (625 gr.) fresh tomatoes, peeled
½ cup olive oil
2 tablespoons dried breadcrumbs
7 to 8 fresh basil leaves, torn, or 1 tablespoon oregano
1 clove garlic, finely chopped
salt and freshly ground black pepper

1. Cut each tomato into four slices.

2. Grease a round oven dish with 1 tablespoon of the oil, and sprinkle with 1 tablespoon of the breadcrumbs. Cover the bottom with the inner slices of the tomatoes. Sprinkle with some garlic, basil, salt and with a lot of pepper.

3. Preheat the oven to 400°F (Gas Mark 6). Drop the spaghetti into rapidly boiling salted water and drain 2 minutes after the water has come back to the boil. Return the pasta to the pot and toss with 3 ounces of the oil (reserving 1 ounce).

4. Put the spaghetti into the oven dish. Cover with a layer of the outer slices of the tomatoes, the round part upwards. Sprinkle with the remaining breadcrumbs, garlic, basil and salt and pepper. Pour over the remaining oil and bake in the oven for 20 minutes.

The modern finishing touch that I have added is to put the dish under the broiler (grill) for a few minutes, until the tops of the tomatoes are just charred.

Here is a typical recipe of the eighteenth century for *Lagane* (large tagliatelle) cooked in milk.

"Prepare the *sfoglia* and cut it into large strips about one finger in width. Let them dry and cook them in boiling milk, slightly salted. Drain them, but leave some milk dripping from them. Sprinkle over them a great quantity of fresh grated Romano cheese and fresh butter."

I am including a description of a rich *timballo* (pasta pie) which is given in Lampedusa's novel *The Leopard.* It is based on a traditional Sicilian recipe. At a dinner at his country house, the Prince Salina gives his Sicilian guests a monumental dish of macaroni as a first course, knowing quite well that it would be much more appreciated than a soup of foreign origin. This description of the *timballo,* carried into the dining-room on a huge silver platter, is quoted here from the translation by A. Colquhoun: "The burnished gold of the crusts, the fragrance of sugar and cinnamon they exuded, were but preludes to the delights released from the interior when the knife broke the crust: first came a spice laden haze, the chicken livers, hard boiled eggs, sliced ham, chicken and truffles in masses of piping hot, glistening macaroni, to which the meat juice gave an exquisite hue of suède." Actually the hard boiled eggs in the *timballo* were not laid eggs, but the eggs which are found inside the chicken and which have a much more delicate flavor.

Here is the recipe for this supreme *timballo,* which ranks among the most sumptuous creations of the *haute cuisine.*

For 8 persons
1 pound (500 gr.) rigatoni or **penne**
1 chicken, cooked (preferably boiled with vegetables)
4 ounces (125 gr.) chicken livers
4 ounces (125 gr.) prosciutto (raw ham), cut into thin
    strips
2 hard boiled eggs, cut into segments
1 cup (100 gr.) Parmesan cheese, freshly grated
1 cup roast meat juice (see recipe for "Macaroni with sauce
    made from pot roast juices" on page 161)
8 tablespoons (125 gr.) butter
1 cup oil for frying
1 white truffle, grated
1 teaspoon cinnamon
1 tablespoon all-purpose (plain) flour
1 tablespoon parsley, chopped
a sweet pastry made with 3¾ cups (500 gr.) all-purpose
    (plain) flour, ¾ cup (190 gr.) butter and ¾ cup
    (75 gr.) sugar
salt and freshly ground black pepper
egg yolk

Sicilian *timballo* from *The Leopard*
Il *timballo del Gattopardo*

1. Bone the cooked chicken, and mince about 8 ounces (250 gr.) of the brown meat.
2. In a bowl combine the chicken mince with the egg, ¾ cup of the Parmesan, the parsley, and salt and pepper. Mix thoroughly, and with this mixture form balls, about the size of a small nut. Flour them very lightly and fry them in the oil for 5 minutes. Lift them out and lay them on paper towels to dry.
3. Cut the breast of the chicken into thin strips.
4. Clean, blanch and chop the chicken livers.
5. Warm the roast juices, sprinkle with the flour, and cook rapidly for 1 to 2 minutes. Add the chicken breast, chicken livers and prosciutto, and cook gently, for a few minutes. The sauce should be thick and velvety. Add the cinnamon, truffle, and adjust seasoning.
6. Drop the macaroni into rapidly boiling salted water.
7. Make two discs from the sweet pastry, one larger than the other, to fit a tin of 9 inches diameter. Butter

the tin and lay the larger disc over the bottom and up the sides of the tin.

8. Preheat the oven to 400°F (Gas Mark 6).

9. Drain the macaroni when very *al dente.* Toss it with the butter, dress with the chicken and ham sauce and sprinkle with the remaining Parmesan.

10. Fill the tin with half the pasta. Make a well in the center, and put into it the meat balls and hard boiled eggs. Cover with the remaining pasta and then with the smaller disc of pastry. Make some holes all over the top with a fork and brush with egg yolk. Bake in the oven for about 1 hour, or until the pastry is cooked.

Timballo of spaghetti with smoked salmon
Timballo di spaghetti alla Bekendorf

This delicious dish is attributed to Bekendorf, who was the head chef of the Tzar Nicholas II.

For 4 to 6 persons.
12 ounces (350 gr.) spaghetti
6 ounces (190 gr.) smoked salmon, cut into strips
½ cup (50 gr.) Parmesan cheese, freshly grated
½ cup (50 gr.) mild Dutch cheese, cut into thin slices
a pinch of nutmeg
6 tablespoons (90 gr.) butter
Béchamel sauce made with 2½ cups of milk (see page 113)
salt and freshly ground black pepper

1. Preheat the oven to 350°F (Gas Mark 4).

2. Make the Béchamel and add the grated nutmeg.

3. Drop the spaghetti into rapidly boiling salted water and drain when very *al dente.*

4. Melt 5 tablespoons (75 gr.) of the butter and pour over the spaghetti.

5. Put one-third of the pasta into a buttered oven dish, cover with half of the salmon strips, half of the sliced cheese and 3 tablespoons of Béchamel. Repeat these layers, finishing with the pasta. Cover with the remaining Béchamel, sprinkle with the Parmesan and dot with the rest of the butter. Bake in the oven for 15 minutes. If you wish, run it under the broiler (grill) until the top is golden brown. Allow to settle for 5 minutes before serving.

In the United States pasta was first introduced by Thomas Jefferson and then gained in popularity in the second half of the nineteenth century with the arrival of the Italian immigrants; in England it arrived through French cooking, rather than directly from Italy.

One of the first recipes to appear in England came from *The Cook's Paradise* by William Verral published in 1759. Verral was an innkeeper, who learned his art as a boy under the great chef St. Clouet. In his book Verral includes two sweet pasta recipes and the following savory one, which is a forerunner of our pasticci. I am indebted to Elizabeth David for drawing my attention to this book.

Macaroni with Parmesan cheese

"These are to be had at any confectioner's in London and the newer they are the better – this is not what we call macaroons of the sweet biscuit sort, but a foreign paste, the same as vermicelly, but made very large in comparison to that – for this you must boil them in water first, with a little salt, pour on them a ladle of coulis, a morsel of green onion and parsley minced fine, pepper, salt and nutmeg: stew all a few minutes, and pour into a dish with a rim, squeeze a lemon or orange, and cover it pretty thick with Parmesan cheese grated very fine, bake it of a fine colour, about a quarter of an hour, and serve it up hot."

My suggested ingredients for 4 persons are:
12 ounces (350 gr.) macaroni
½ cup of meat juices (see page 160) thickened with 1
teaspoon all-purpose (plain) flour
4 tablespoons (60 gr.) butter
1 tablespoon onion
parsley
salt and pepper and nutmeg
¾ cup (75 gr.) freshly grated Parmesan cheese
the grated rind and juice of ½ lemon or orange

In the nineteenth century pasta began to grow in popularity. The variety of ways in which it was served depended as much on economic circumstances as on climatic differences. In Italy, pasta was rapidly becoming the staple food of the masses, but the upper classes of England and America were serving most of their macaroni dishes as "nursery food" for their children. They were usually bland, sweet puddings which the children loved because they were warming and easy to chew.

From a nineteenth-century English cookbook:

Baked vermicelli

"Simmer 4 ounces of vermicelli in a pint of new milk 10 minutes. Then put to it $\frac{1}{2}$ pint of cream, a teaspoonful of pounded cinnamon, 4 ounces of butter warmed, the same of white sugar, and the yolks of 4 eggs well beaten: a little oil of almonds or a couple of spoonfuls of ratafia will much improve the flavour. Bake in a dish without lining: but observe that of the two sorts of vermicelli the Genoese will require $\frac{3}{4}$ and the Neapolitan only $\frac{1}{2}$ an hour of baking."

Boiled vermicelli

"Stir very gently 4 ounces of vermicelli into a pint of new milk over the stove, until it be scalding hot, but not more: then pour it into a basin and add to it, while hot, 1 ounce of butter and 2 of sugar. When the above is nearly cold, mix in, very gently, 2 well-beaten eggs: and immediately put it into a basin which will exactly hold it. Cover carefully with a floured cloth: and turning the basin the narrow end upwards, move it around for 10 minutes and boil for an hour. Serve with pudding sauce."

From a nineteenth-century American cookbook:

Baked macaroni

"Simmer 1 or 2 ounces of the pipe sort in 2 cups of milk, and a bit of lemon and cinnamon, till tender: put it into a dish with the milk, 2 or 3 yolks of eggs, but only 1 white, sugar, nutmeg, 1 spoonful of peach-water or almond and a glass of raisin wine. Bake with a paste round the edges.

A layer of orange marmalade or raspberry jam at the bottom of a macaroni pudding, for change, is a great improvement, in which case omit the almond or peach-water, which you would otherwise flavor it with, or a glass of brandy."

A savory nursery dish of 1860:

Vegetable pie

"Boil some vermicelli and strain it. Have some onions chopped fine, and fry until slightly brown in a little butter. Have some eggs hard boiled and some tomatoes cut in slices. Put a layer of tomatoes in the bottom of a pie dish, then some onions and a layer of eggs, cut in slices. Then the vermicelli. Cover with some 'nice white sauce' and a little chopped parsley, picked fresh from the herb garden, and on the top of all some slices of potatoes. Put in the oven and bake for about half an hour until the potatoes are brown on the top."

As you have read, pasta was often a "pudding" up to the eighteenth century in Italy and even later in America and in England. There are also a few Central European recipes of pasta puddings. In Italy too there are still some sweet pasta dishes, such as "Macaroni with chocolate sauce," a traditional dish from Orvieto in Umbria. I have tried it, but I found it quite unpalatable and therefore I could not possibly work out a recipe for it. I am including, however, four sweet dishes, which I found very pleasant, interesting and unusual in taste and appearance. You might like to try them too, and you will realize that pasta is certainly one of the most versatile foods.

This is an old Rumanian recipe, a delicious and esoteric pudding which should be made with homemade noodles.

Sweet noodles with raisins and almonds
Cataif

For 6 to 8 persons
*Homemade noodles made with 2 eggs and 1¾ cups (250
    gr.) all-purpose (plain) flour and 2 tablespoons water
    (see page 102)*
½ cup (90 gr.) raisins (sultanas)
¼ cup (45 gr.) mixed peel
1 cup (100 gr.) almonds, blanched, toasted and chopped
grated rind and juice of 1 lemon
6 tablespoons (90 gr.) butter
2 teaspoons cinnamon
3 tablespoons (45 gr.) sugar
salt
caramel topping made with ½ cup sugar and ¼ cup water
heavy (double) cream

1. Drop the noodles into rapidly boiling water to which only 1 tablespoon of salt has been added. Drain the pasta 2 minutes after it has come back to the boil. Toss with 4 tablespoons (60 gr.) of the butter and sprinkle with the cinnamon.
2. Preheat the oven to 300°F (Gas Mark 2).
3. Pour one-third of the noodles into a buttered oven dish, cover with half the raisins, almonds, mixed peel, lemon rind and sugar. Repeat these layers, and finish with noodles. Bake in the oven for 15 minutes.
4. While the pasta is baking, make the caramel

topping. Put the sugar into a dry saucepan, and stir over low heat until the sugar melts and turns a golden brown. Take off the heat and add the water. Take care since the mixture will boil furiously when the cold water is added. Return the pan to the heat, and stir until a syrup is formed. Add the lemon juice. Pour this sauce over the pasta, and bake the pudding for a further 5 minutes. Serve with heavy (double) cream on the side.

Short macaroni with prunes

This is a very old middle-European recipe.

For 6 persons
8 ounces (250 gr.) short pasta
1 cup (200 gr.) dried prunes, pitted
6 tablespoons (90 gr.) butter
¼ cup (50 gr.) sugar
1 teaspoon cinnamon
2 cloves
salt.
heavy (double) cream

1. Soak the prunes, if necessary. Cover them with cold water, add the cinnamon and cloves and cook until tender. Remove the cloves.
2. Preheat the oven to 300°F (Gas Mark 2).
3. Drop the pasta into rapidly boiling water to which only 1 tablespoon of salt has been added. Cook the pasta for 5 more minutes after it is *al dente*. Drain, reserving some of the water in which it has cooked.
4. Turn the pasta into a buttered oven dish, add the prunes, butter, sugar and approximately ½ cup of the water. Mix thoroughly, cover with foil and bake for 15 minutes. Serve with heavy (double) cream on the side.

Noodle and apple cake
Lokshen scholent

This is a traditional Jewish pudding which originated in Germany, but is also quite well known in Poland.

The *sfoglia* should not be rolled as thin as for Italian tagliatelle.

For 6 persons
Homemade noodles made with 2 eggs and 1½ cups
all-purpose (plain) flour (see page 102)
6 tablespoons (60 gr.) all-purpose (plain) flour
½ teaspoon baking soda
¾ cup (75 gr.) sugar
½ cup (90 gr.) raisins
6 tablespoons (90 gr.) butter

3 eggs
½ cup milk
¼ teaspoon cinnamon
½ pound eating apples, peeled and sliced
Heavy (double) cream.

1. Preheat the oven to 350°F (Gas Mark 4).
2. Cook the noodles in slightly salted boiling water
and drain them 1 minute after the water has come back
to the boil, reserving ½ cup of the water.
3. Toss the pasta with the reserved water, 4
tablespoons (60 gr.) of the butter, and the milk. Mix in
the sugar, flour and cinnamon. Stir thoroughly, add the
raisins, and stir again.
4. Separate the egg yolks from the whites. Beat the
yolks with a fork, and add to the pasta mixture.
5. Whip the whites of the eggs and fold gently into the
mixture.
6. Fill a buttered, deep oven dish with half of the
mixture. Lay the apple slices on top and cover with the
remaining mixture. Dot with the remaining butter,
cover with foil, and bake in the oven for approximately
¾ hour. Serve with lots of heavy (double) cream.

Sweet macaroni with raisins
Tortino di maccheroncini con le uvette

For 6 persons
8 ounces (250 gr.) elbow macaroni
1¼ cups milk
4 tablespoons (60 gr.) butter
⅓ cup (60 gr.) raisins (sultanas)
¼ cup (50 gr.) sugar
1 teaspoon cinnamon
1 egg yolk
½ cup light (single) cream
1 teaspoon salt
2 tablespoons brandy
heavy (double) cream

1. Soak the raisins in the brandy.
2. Boil the milk. Add the pasta, butter and salt; cover,
and simmer very gently until all the milk has been
absorbed (approximately ¾ hour). Cool slightly.
3. Preheat the oven to 300°F (Gas Mark 2).
4. Beat into the pasta pudding the egg yolk, cinnamon,
raisins, cream and sugar.
5. Pour the mixture into a buttered oven dish, cover
with foil and bake for approximately ½ hour. Serve
with some heavy (double) cream on the side.

Modern recipes

Here are 40 modern recipes. Most of them can be made very quickly, although some are easier than others. I have arranged them according to the ingredients of the sauce: dairy products sauces, sauces with eggs, with vegetables, with fish, and with meat and poultry.

Almost all the recipes have been designed as first courses, but the ingredients can be increased when the dishes are to be served as main courses.

Spaghetti with butter
Spaghetti all'inglese

For 4 persons
12 ounces (350 gr.) spaghetti
8 tablespoons (125 gr.) butter
1 cup (100 gr.) Parmesan cheese, freshly grated
salt and freshly ground black pepper

1. Cook and drain the spaghetti and pour it into a hot dish.
2. Cut the butter into small lumps and add it to the pasta mixing rapidly. Sprinkle with lots of pepper and half of the cheese. Serve at once with the remaining cheese on the side.

Variations:

I. Melt 1 teaspoon of meat extract with 1 tablespoon of the water in which the pasta was boiled and pour it over the pasta dressed with the butter and cheese.

II. Melt the butter together with a few torn fresh sage leaves and one clove of garlic, whole or crushed. Sauté the garlic and sage very gently until just golden, taking care not to burn them as this would give a bitter taste. Pour over the drained spaghetti, first removing the garlic if a whole clove has been used. Serve with the Parmesan on the side.

Spaghetti with cream
Spaghetti alla panna fresca

For 4 persons
12 ounces (350 gr.) spaghetti
4 tablespoons (60 gr.) butter
½ cup heavy (double) cream
½ cup (50 gr.) Parmesan cheese, freshly grated
salt and freshly ground black pepper

1. Drop the spaghetti into rapidly boiling salted water.
2. In a serving bowl combine the cream and half the cheese and place in a cool oven (280°F – Gas Mark ½) for 5 minutes.
3. Drain the pasta and turn it into the bowl with the cream and cheese, adding the butter and lots of pepper. Mix thoroughly. Serve with the rest of the cheese on the side.

Spaghetti with cream and onion
Spaghetti alla panna fresca con cipolla

For 4 persons
12 ounces (350 gr.) spaghetti
4 tablespoons (60 gr.) butter
½ cup heavy (double) cream
1 tablespoon all-purpose (plain) flour

1 small onion, grated
1 tablespoon parsley
pinch of nutmeg
freshly grated Parmesan cheese
salt and freshly ground black pepper

1. Drop the spaghetti into rapidly boiling salted water.
2. Melt half of the butter in a frying pan, add the flour and onion and sauté for 5 minutes.
3. When the onion begins to soften, add the cream, nutmeg, salt and pepper, and parsley and cook, stirring constantly, for 1 minute. Pour the sauce into a warm serving bowl and keep it warm.
4. Drain the spaghetti, turn it into the bowl with the sauce and add the rest of the butter. Mix and serve with the Parmesan on the side.

Spaghetti with oil and garlic
Spaghetti con olio e aglio

For 4 persons
12 ounces (350 gr.) spaghetti or vermicelli
6 tablespoons olive oil
3 cloves garlic
3 tablespoons parsley, chopped
salt and freshly ground black pepper

1. Put the oil into a large frying pan, and when it is hot, add the parsley, the crushed or finely chopped garlic, and lots of black pepper. Sauté for 2 to 3 minutes.
2. Cook and drain the pasta when still very *al dente*. Add it to the oil and garlic, and cook for 2 minutes, stirring constantly. Be careful not to burn the garlic, as it would give a bitter taste. Serve at once. No cheese is needed.

Vermicelli with fancy tomato sauce
Vermicelli con salsa rossa

For 4 persons
12 ounces (350 gr.) vermicelli
1 pound (500 gr.) fresh tomatoes, peeled, or canned plum
*   tomatoes*
4 tablespoons (60 gr.) butter
2 ounces (60 gr.) ham, diced
1 small onion, finely chopped
4 to 5 leaves fresh basil, torn, or 2 tablespoons parsley,
*   chopped*
salt and freshly ground black pepper
freshly grated Parmesan cheese

139

1. Purée the tomatoes through a food mill.
2. In a large frying pan sauté the onion and ham in half the butter for approximately 5 minutes.
3. Drop the vermicelli into rapidly boiling salted water.
4. Add the tomato purée to the sauce and boil rapidly for 5 minutes, stirring occasionally. Add the basil or parsley and adjust seasoning.
5. Drain the pasta when very *al dente*. Toss with the remaining butter and add to the sauce. Fry for 2 minutes, stirring constantly. Serve with the Parmesan on the side.

Spaghetti with vegetable margarine
Spaghetti alla margarina vegetale

This dressing is ideal for those who prefer not to eat butter for health reasons, but do not like the taste of olive oil.

For 4 persons
12 ounces (350 gr.) spaghetti
12 tablespoons (180 gr.) margarine*
salt and freshly ground black pepper
1 teaspoon meat extract.

1. Cook and drain the spaghetti (reserving a little of the cooking liquid) and pour it into a hot dish.
2. Cut the margarine into small lumps and add it to the pasta, mixing rapidly. Dissolve the meat extract into 1 tablespoon of the water in which the spaghetti was cooked and pour it over the pasta. Sprinkle with a good quantity of black pepper.

Variation:

Melt the margarine together with a few torn fresh sage leaves, one clove of garlic (whole or crushed) and one hot red pepper. Sauté the garlic very gently until just golden. Remove the garlic and the hot pepper and pour the sauce over the drained spaghetti.

Spaghetti with Gorgonzola and ricotta
Spaghetti con Gorgonzola e ricotta

The making of this sauce requires a blender.

For 4 persons
12 ounces (350 gr.) spaghetti
2 ounces (60 gr.) Gorgonzola cheese
½ cup (90 gr.) ricotta or cottage cheese

* In the United States I would recommend Fleischmanns Margarine or Promise, in Britain Flora.

4 tablespoons light (single) cream
4 tablespoons (60 gr.) butter
1 small celery stick, chopped
½ clove garlic, chopped
salt and freshly ground black pepper

1. Put the cheeses and cream in a blender and blend until soft and creamy (add more cream if necessary). Add the celery, garlic and plenty of black pepper.
2. Cook and drain the spaghetti, reserving 2 tablespoons of the water in which it was cooked. Turn the spaghetti into a warm serving dish, toss with the butter, and then add the sauce and the reserved water. Mix thoroughly and serve at once.

Variation:
   Instead of garlic and pepper use 1 tablespoon of chopped onion and 1 heaped teaspoon of paprika.

   Sir Winston Churchill was apparently very fond of this sauce.

Spaghetti with prosciutto and cheeses
Spaghetti alla Churchill

For 4 persons
12 ounces (350 gr.) spaghetti
2 ounces (60 gr.) smoked
   cheese, diced
2 ounces (60 gr.) Gruyère
   cheese, diced
½ cup (50 gr.) Parmesan
   cheese, freshly grated
4 ounces (125 gr.) prosciutto (raw
   ham), cut into Julienne strips
a Béchamel sauce made with 1¼ cups milk, 2
   tablespoons (30 gr.) butter and 2 tablespoons (20 gr.)
   all-purpose (plain) flour (see page 113)
4 tablespoons (60 gr.) butter
salt and freshly ground black pepper

1. Drop the spaghetti into rapidly boiling salted water.
2. Over very low heat, melt the diced cheeses in the Béchamel. Add the prosciutto and keep warm.
3. Place the butter in a serving bowl and put it into a cool oven (280°F – Gas Mark ½) for 2 to 3 minutes to melt.
4. Drain the spaghetti, turn into the serving bowl with the butter and cover with the Béchamel. Serve with the Parmesan on the side.

Small shells with Gorgonzola, pistachios and brandy
Conchigliette con salsa di Gorgonzola, pistacchi e cognac

This sauce is made up of some unlikely ingredients, but the result is really food for the Gods.

For 4 persons
12 ounces (350 gr.) small shells
3 ounces (90 gr.) Gorgonzola cheese
8 tablespoons (125 gr.) butter
2 tablespoons pistachio nuts, shelled
2 tablespoons brandy
½ cup light (single) cream
salt and freshly ground black pepper

1. Put the pistachio nuts in a small bowl and cover with boiling water. Let stand for two minutes, and then peel. Pound the nuts with a mortar and pestle.
2. Drop the pasta into rapidly boiling salted water.
3. In the top half of a double boiler, or in a heavy-bottomed saucepan over very low heat, melt the butter with the cheese. As soon as they have melted, add the cream, and cook very gently for 5 minutes, stirring continuously.
4. Remove from heat and add pistachio nuts and brandy. Pour over the drained pasta and mix thoroughly. Serve at once.

Open-faced spaghetti omelette
Frittata di spaghetti

The Italian omelette is always open-faced, like a Spanish *tortilla*. This particular variety is very economical since it can be made with left-over spaghetti which has already been dressed with butter and cheese, or with tomato sauce.

For 4 persons
12 ounces (350 gr.) spaghetti
4 tablespoons (60 gr.) butter
2 tablespoons olive oil (good corn oil would do)
2 eggs
2 tablespoons parsley, chopped
½ cup (50 gr.) Parmesan or mild Cheddar cheese, grated
salt and freshly ground black pepper

1. If there is no left-over spaghetti, cook and drain the spaghetti, and dress it with the butter and half of the cheese. Set aside to cool, stirring occasionally to prevent the pasta from sticking.
2. Add the eggs, the rest of the cheese, the parsley and salt and pepper to the spaghetti. Mix very thoroughly.
3. Heat the oil in a large heavy-bottomed frying pan.

When it is hot, add the spaghetti mixture, and spread it evenly. Cook over low heat, using a wooden spatula to prevent it from sticking, for approximately 15 minutes.
4. Place the pan under the broiler (grill) for about 1 minute, or until the top side of the omelette is cooked and just golden. Let it cool slightly before sliding it onto a warm serving dish. Cut into wedges and serve.

Nobody knows where this sauce got its name. It has no apparent relation to coal (*carbone*), and there is no record of its being created by the *Carbonari,* a secret sect who fought for the independence of Italy during the Risorgimento. Whatever its origin, *spaghetti alla Carbonara* became a very popular dish in Italy after the second world war. This is presumably because it was loved by the Allied Troops since it combines their old favorites, bacon and eggs.

Bucatini with eggs and bacon
Bucatini alla Carbonara

For 4 persons
12 ounces (350 gr.) **bucatini** *or elbow macaroni*
1 cup (100 gr.) unsmoked lean bacon,
cut into Julienne strips
4 egg yolks
4 tablespoons (60 gr.) butter
1 tablespoon olive oil (good vegetable oil can be used)
1 cup (100 gr.) Parmesan cheese, freshly grated (or ½ cup
Parmesan and ½ cup good strong Cheddar)
2 tablespoons all-purpose cream
salt and freshly ground black pepper

1. Sauté the bacon in the oil over low heat for 10 minutes or until it is turning brown.
2. Drop the pasta into a saucepan of boiling salted water.
3. While the pasta is cooking, beat together the cheese, egg yolks, salt and lots of black pepper, and cream in a mixing bowl.
4. Melt the butter in a large frying pan and pour into it the egg mixture, the drained pasta and the bacon. Mix thoroughly over low heat for 1 minute. Serve at once.

The timing of this dish is very important as the eggs must not be allowed to over-cook. Make sure the pasta is just ready when the butter is being melted, and do not over-drain it.
A safer method is to gently warm the butter and the egg mixture in the serving bowl in a cool oven, which

143

will enable the eggs to cook enough without scrambling. When the pasta is done, toss it in the mixture, and add the bacon.

Variations:
  I. Butter can be substituted for the cream.
  II. 4 or 5 fresh sage leaves can be torn and added to the bacon while it is being sautéed.
  III. You can use 3 whole eggs, instead of 4 yolks.

Penne with onions
Penne con salsa di cipolle

For 4 persons
12 ounces (350 gr.) **penne** *or elbow macaroni*
3 good sized onions, sliced very finely
8 tablespoons (125 gr.) butter
1 teaspoon all-purpose (plain) flour
a little meat extract (half a meat cube or Bovril), dissolved
    in 1 tablespoon water
salt and freshly ground black pepper
freshly grated Parmesan cheese (or mild Cheddar)

1. Melt the butter in a small heavy-bottomed saucepan. When the foam subsides, add the onions, and let them sauté very gently for about 10 minutes. Add the flour, meat extract, salt and pepper. Mix thoroughly, squashing the onions against the sides of the pan with a wooden spoon to help release their juices. Cook over very low heat for about 30 minutes, making sure the sauce does not get too dry. It should be golden and of a mushy consistency.
2. While the sauce is cooking, boil the *penne.*
3. Drain the pasta, and turn into a warm serving bowl. Quickly toss in a small lump of butter, and then the sauce. Serve immediately with Parmesan or mild Cheddar cheese.

Vermicelli with curried ham and peas
Vermicelli con prosciutto cotto e piselli al curry

For 4 persons
12 ounces (350 gr.) vermicelli
6 tablespoons (90 gr.) butter
4 ounces (125 gr.) fresh peas or frozen or canned **petits-pois**
4 ounces (125 gr.) ham, cut into matchsticks
3 tablespoons heavy (double) cream
1 to 2 teaspoons curry powder
salt
freshly grated Parmesan cheese

1. Cook and drain the peas.
2. Drop the vermicelli into rapidly boiling salted water.

3. Melt the butter in a large frying pan and sauté the ham for 1 minute. Add curry powder according to taste and cook gently for 1–2 minutes. Add the peas and cream and adjust seasoning. Cook over low heat for 3 minutes, adding 2 or 3 tablespoons of the water in which the pasta is cooking.

4. Drain the pasta when it is very *al dente* and turn it into the frying pan. Fry for 2 minutes, stirring constantly. Serve at once with a bowl of Parmesan on the side.

Tortellini are a smaller version of ravioli, and are rounded rather than square. They can be bought freshly made from many Italian stores in most big cities. Homemade ravioli could be substituted in this recipe (see page 186).

Tortellini with prosciutto and peas
Tortellini della Nonna

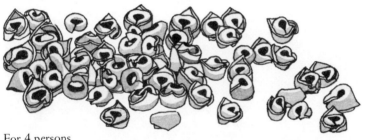

For 4 persons
*14 ounces (420 gr.) fresh **tortellini** or homemade ravioli*
4 ounces (125 gr.) prosciutto (raw ham) or very lean
    unsmoked bacon, cut into matchsticks
4 ounces (125 gr.) cooked peas
8 tablespoons (125 gr.) butter
½ cup heavy (double) cream
1 cup (100 gr.) Parmesan cheese, freshly grated
salt and freshly ground black pepper

1. In a large frying pan combine the butter and prosciutto or bacon and cook over low heat for 5 minutes.

2. Drop the pasta into rapidly boiling salted water. Drain the *tortellini* when they are just tender. The cooking time varies: if fresh they take about 5 minutes, if dry 15 to 20 minutes. Turn them into the frying pan, and mix well to coat them with the butter.

3. Add the peas, cream and half the Parmesan cheese. Sprinkle generously with freshly ground pepper, and serve with the remaining Parmesan on the side.

145

Vermicelli with ham, mushrooms and peas
Vermicelli con prosciutto cotto, funghi e piselli

For 4 persons
12 ounces (350 gr.) vermicelli
4 ounces (125 gr.) mushrooms, finely sliced
3 ounces (90 gr.) ham, cut into matchsticks
3 ounces (90 gr.) fresh peas, shelled, or frozen or canned
  petits-pois
2 tablespoons heavy (double) cream
6 tablespoons (90 gr.) butter
1 clove garlic
salt and freshly ground black pepper
freshly grated Parmesan cheese

1. Cook and drain the peas.
2. In a frying pan, sauté the mushrooms and garlic clove in 4 tablespoons of the butter for approximately 5 minutes.
3. Drop the vermicelli into rapidly boiling salted water.
4. Add the ham and peas to the mushrooms and cook for a further 5 minutes, stirring constantly. Remove garlic clove. Add the cream.
5. Drain the pasta, reserving $\frac{1}{2}$ cup of the water in which it was cooked. Turn the vermicelli into a warm serving dish, toss it with the remaining butter and then stir in the hot water. Pour over the sauce and serve immediately, with a bowl of Parmesan on the side.

Tagliolini with asparagus
Tagliolini con gli asparagi

For 4 persons
Homemade pasta made with $2\frac{1}{4}$ cups (300 gr.) all-purpose (plain) flour and 3 eggs or 12 ounces (350 gr.) dry **tagliolini**
1 pound (500 gr.) asparagus, preferably fresh
6 tablespoons (90 gr.) butter
$\frac{1}{2}$ cup light (single) cream
2 tablespoons onion, grated
a pinch of nutmeg
salt and freshly ground black pepper
freshly grated Parmesan cheese

1. If you are making the pasta at home follow the instructions on page 102 and leave the *tagliolini* to dry for at least 15 minutes.
2. Lightly scrape the asparagus stalks and wash them in cold water. Tie the asparagus into small bundles and immerse them in rapidly boiling salted water. Boil them, uncovered, for 10 to 15 minutes, or until barely tender. Drain, reserving the water in which they were

cooked. Cut off the tips (the top $1\frac{1}{2}$ inches) for use in this recipe. The stalks may be used in a soup or a mousse.

3. If you are using dry *tagliolini*, drop it into rapidly boiling lightly salted water to which you have added the cooking water from the asparagus. If you are using homemade pasta, make the sauce first and keep it warm while you boil the *tagliolini* in plain water to which you have added the asparagus water.

4. Melt the butter in a frying pan, add the onion and cook for about 5 minutes. Add the cream, asparagus tips, nutmeg, salt and a good quantity of pepper. Mix gently, taking care not to break the tips.

5. Drain the pasta and turn it into a warm serving bowl. Pour over the sauce, and serve with a bowl of Parmesan on the side.

Variation:
    Add 2 ounces (60 gr.) diced ham to the butter and fry for 5 minutes before adding the onion. Proceed as above.

Thin spaghetti with leeks
Spaghettini con i porri

For 4 persons
*12 ounces (350 gr.) thin spaghetti, vermicelli or **tagliolini***
2 pounds (1000 gr.) leeks
8 tablespoons (125 gr.) butter
2 tablespoons light (single) cream
1 teaspoon curry powder
$\frac{1}{2}$ cup meat stock
1 cup (100 gr.) Parmesan cheese, freshly grated
salt and freshly ground black pepper

1. Cut the white part of the leeks into very thin rings and wash very thoroughly until the water is absolutely clear. (You can use the rest of the leek for soup.)

2. In a large frying pan, melt the butter and add the leeks. Add the curry powder and cook over very low heat for about 30 minutes. Add the meat stock during the cooking to prevent the sauce from getting too thick. It should be of a mushy consistency. Adjust seasoning.

3. Drop the pasta into rapidly boiling salted water. Drain when still very *al dente*, reserving $\frac{1}{2}$ cup of the cooking water.

4. Turn the pasta into the frying pan, add the cream, the remaining butter, half the Parmesan and some of the water. Mix thoroughly over low heat for 2 minutes and serve at once with the remaining Parmesan on the side.

147

Fusilli with dried mushrooms, parsley and cream sauce
Fusilli con salsa di funghi secchi, prezzemolo e panna

For 4 persons
12 ounces (350 gr.) fusilli or spaghetti
½ ounce (15 gr.) dried mushrooms
4 tablespoons (60 gr.) butter
½ cup chopped parsley
1 clove garlic, finely chopped
½ cup light (single) cream
salt and freshly ground black pepper

1. In a small bowl, soak the mushrooms in warm water for 1 hour. Remove, retaining about ½ cup of the water for the sauce, and chop coarsely.
2. In a frying pan large enough to hold the pasta, melt the butter. Add the parsley, cream, and garlic and cook over low heat for 1 minute, stirring constantly. Add the mushroom pieces and continue to simmer for 10 minutes, adding between ¼ to ½ cup of the water in which the mushrooms were soaked. Adjust seasoning.
3. Drop the pasta into rapidly boiling salted water. Drain when very *al dente,* and turn into the frying pan. Cook for 2 minutes, stirring constantly.

This sauce is usually served without cheese, but you may wish to pass a bowl of grated Parmesan on the side.

Vermicelli with anchovy, garlic and parsley sauce
Vermicelli con Salsa di Acciuga

For 4 persons
12 ounces (350 gr.) vermicelli or thin spaghetti
2 ounces (60 gr.) anchovy fillets
2 cloves garlic, chopped
5 tablespoons olive oil
3 tablespoons parsley, chopped
salt and freshly ground black pepper

1. Drop the vermicelli into rapidly boiling salted water.
2. Gently heat the oil and garlic in a frying pan for 2 to 3 minutes. Add the anchovies and mash them with a fork until a thick paste is formed. Add parsley and pepper to taste.
3. Drain the vermicelli, turn into a warm serving dish and pour the sauce over it, mixing thoroughly. Serve.
No cheese is needed.

Variation:

Drain the pasta when very *al dente* and turn it into the frying pan. Fry over moderate heat for 1 minute, mixing rapidly with a fork.

This sauce derives its name from its Sicilian origin.

**Fusilli with anchovy
fillets and black olives**
Fusilli alla Mafia

For 4 persons
12 ounces (350 gr.) fusilli
*2 ounces (60 gr.) black olives, stoned and cut into small
    strips*
2 ounces (60 gr.) anchovy fillets, chopped
2 cloves garlic, finely chopped
5 tablespoons olive oil
the rind of a lemon, in 1 or 2 pieces
4 tablespoons parsley, chopped
*½ or 1 hot red chili pepper, crumbled, more or less according
    to taste*
freshly grated Romano or Parmesan cheese
salt

1. Leave the olive oil and lemon rind to marinate in a
large frying pan for about 30 minutes.
2. Drop the *fusilli* into rapidly boiling salted water.
3. While the pasta is cooking, heat the frying pan over
low heat. When the oil is hot add the anchovies, and
mash them with a fork as they cook. add the garlic, red
hot pepper, olives, parsley and salt. Mix thoroughly
and fry for 2 to 3 minutes. Remove lemon rind.
4. Drain the pasta when it is very *al dente*. Turn it into
the frying pan and cook for a further 2 minutes, stirring
constantly. Serve with a bowl of Romano or Parmesan
cheese on the side.

This sauce is very easy and quick to make, an ideal
after theater supper. You need not use the very
expensive sturgeon caviar.

Spaghetti with caviar
Spaghetti al caviale

For 4 persons
12 ounces (350 gr.) spaghetti
4 tablespoons (60 gr.) butter
2 ounces (60 gr.) caviar
2 tablespoons cottage cheese
2 tablespoons heavy (double) cream
freshly ground black pepper

1. In a large frying pan, melt the butter and add the
cheese, cream, and lots of black pepper. Cook for 2
minutes.
2. Drop the spaghetti into rapidly boiling salted water.
3. Add the caviar to the cream mixture and stir well to
form a smooth paste.

149

4. Drain the pasta when very *al dente*, reserving 2 tablespoons of the water. Turn the spaghetti into the frying pan, add the water, and fry for 1 minute, stirring constantly. Serve without cheese.

Thin spaghetti with tuna fish sauce
Spaghettini con salsa di tonno

For 4 persons
12 ounces (350 gr.) thin spaghetti or linguine
7 ounces (210 gr.) canned tuna fish, the sort packed in olive oil, drained
4 tablespoons olive oil
1 pound (500 gr.) fresh tomatoes, peeled, or canned plum tomatoes
4 ounces (125 gr.) black olives, stoned
2 ounces (60 gr.) capers
1 very small onion, chopped
2 cloves garlic, finely chopped
1 small stick celery, chopped
fresh basil or parsley
salt and freshly ground black pepper

1. Sauté the onion and garlic in the oil until transparent.
2. Add the tomatoes and cook for 5 minutes. Add the shredded tuna, capers, olives, celery, torn basil leaves or chopped parsley, and simmer for 10 minutes.
3. While the sauce is cooking, cook and drain the pasta. Turn it into a serving bowl, and cover with the sauce. Serve. No cheese is needed.

Thin spaghetti with haddock fillets
Spaghettini con filetti di nasello

For 4 persons
12 ounces (350 gr.) thin spaghetti
12 ounces (350 gr.) haddock fillets
12 ounces (350 gr.) fresh tomatoes, peeled, or canned plum tomatoes
4 anchovy fillets
½ cup olive oil
2 tablespoons (30 gr.) butter
1 clove garlic, finely chopped
a few sprigs of parsley, chopped
1 small hot red chili pepper
salt and freshly ground black pepper

1. Skin the haddock and cut it into small pieces.
2. Over low heat, combine the oil, garlic, anchovy fillets, and pound them to a paste. Add the haddock and whole hot red pepper. Adjust seasoning.
3. Purée the tomatoes and add them to the sauce.

Cook over moderately high heat for 10 minutes.
4. While the sauce is cooking, drop the pasta into
rapidly boiling salted water.
5. Remove the hot pepper from the sauce and add the
parsley. Mix well.
6. Drain the pasta and turn it into a warm serving
bowl. Toss with butter, cover with the sauce and serve.
No cheese is needed.

Spaghetti with shrimp and curry sauce
Spaghetti con salsa di gamberetti e curry

For 4 persons
12 ounces (350 gr.) spaghetti
6 ounces (180 gr.) fresh or frozen shrimp, shelled
6 tablespoons (90 gr.) butter
2 egg yolks
4 tablespoons heavy (double) cream
½ cup dry white wine
curry powder to taste
salt
freshly grated Parmesan cheese (optional)

1. Sauté the shrimp gently in 4 tablespoons of the
butter for a few minutes. If you are using fresh shrimp
add ½ cup of water. When they begin to get dry, add
the wine. Raise heat and boil rapidly until liquid is
reduced by more than half.
2. Reduce heat and add curry powder (1 tablespoon is
the average dose). Mix well.
3. Cook and drain the spaghetti. Turn it into the top
of a double boiler and quickly mix in the rest of the
butter, the cream and the egg yolks. Cook for 1–2
minutes *over*, not in, boiling water. Add the shrimp
sauce. Mix and serve at once. The cheese may be added
to the spaghetti with the cream or passed around the
table separately.

Linguine with shrimp and peas
Linguine con salsa di gamberetti e piselli

For 4 persons
12 ounces (350 gr.) linguine or flat macaroni
8 ounces (250 gr.) fresh or frozen shrimp
8 ounces (250 gr.) fresh peas or frozen or canned petits-pois
6 tablespoons (90 gr.) butter
1 tablespoon grated onion
1 teaspoon all-purpose (plain) flour
2 tablespoons white wine
2 egg yolks
2 tablespoons heavy (double) cream
2 drops Tabasco
salt

1. Melt 4 tablespoons (60 gr.) of the butter in a heavy-bottomed frying pan. Add the grated onion and the flour. Mix well and cook for 2 to 3 minutes.
2. If you are using fresh peas, cook them until barely tender by simmering them, covered, in ½ cup water with 2 tablespoons butter for about 20 minutes. For frozen peas, follow the directions on the package. If fresh shrimp are used, they should be shelled, and a bit of water should be added with them to the sauce. Add the shrimp and cooked peas to the butter and onion mixture. After about 1 minute add the wine. Boil rapidly for 5 minutes, stirring constantly. Adjust seasoning.
3. While the sauce is cooking, drop the pasta into rapidly boiling salted water.
4. 2 minutes before the pasta is done, remove the sauce from the heat and beat in the egg yolks, cream and Tabasco.
5. Drain the pasta. Turn into a warm serving bowl, toss with the remaining butter and cover with the sauce. Serve at once. If you wish, you can serve a bowl of grated Parmesan on the side.

Spaghetti with smoked cod's roe
Spaghetti con uova di pesce affumicate

The making of this sauce requires a blender.
For 4 persons
12 ounces (350 gr.) spaghetti
4 ounces (125 gr.) smoked cod's roe
5 tablespoons olive oil
5 tablespoons heavy (double) cream
a good-sized sprig of parsley
2 tablespoons (30 gr.) butter
1 clove garlic
freshly ground black pepper

1. Peel the roe and discard all the red outer skin.
2. Combine all the ingredients except the butter and spaghetti in the blender to form a smooth paste.
3. Cook and drain the spaghetti, reserving ½ cup of the water in which it was cooked. Transfer the pasta to a warm dish and dress with the butter. Mix well.
4. Pour over the sauce and mix again. If it seems too dry add a bit of the hot water in which the pasta was cooked. Serve immediately. No cheese is needed.

Variation:

For a slightly hotter taste, a few drops of Tabasco may be added instead of the black pepper.

For 4 persons
12 ounces (350 gr.) spaghetti
8 ounces (250 gr.) soft roes
*8 ounces (250 gr.) fresh tomatoes, peeled, or canned plum
    tomatoes*
2 cloves garlic, finely chopped
2 tablespoons parsley, chopped
4 tablespoons olive oil
salt and freshly ground black pepper
4 tablespoons heavy (double) cream (optional)

Spaghetti with soft roes
Spaghetti con uova di aringhe

1. Heat the oil in a heavy-bottomed frying pan. Add
the finely sliced tomatoes and the garlic and sauté for 8
to 10 minutes.
2. Add the roes and cook gently for about 10 minutes,
breaking them up with a wooden spoon. Correct
seasoning. Just before serving, stir in the parsley and the
cream.
3. Cook and drain the spaghetti. Turn it into a hot
dish, toss it with a little olive oil and then cover with
the sauce. Serve at once. No cheese is needed.

This sauce is called "*alla pizzaiola*" because it is
reminiscent of the filling of the original Neapolitan
pizza.

Spaghetti with pizza sauce
Spaghetti alla pizzaiola

For 4 persons
12 ounces (350 gr.) spaghetti
*1 pound (500 gr.) chuck steak**
*1 pound (500 gr.) fresh tomatoes, peeled, or canned plum
    tomatoes*
2 cloves garlic, finely chopped
2 tablespoons (30 gr.) capers
2 tablespoons olive oil
2 tablespoons (30 gr.) butter
3 tablespoons fresh parsley, chopped
salt and freshly ground black pepper

1. Cut the meat into thin slices, and then into strips 2
inches long by $\frac{1}{2}$ inch wide. Heat the butter with 1
tablespoon of the oil in a large deep frying pan. When
the foam subsides, add the strips of meat and brown

---

* You can serve the meat in the spaghetti sauce or you may wish to
serve it as a second course accompanied by fresh spinach or sautéed
zucchini (courgettes). In this case, lift the meat out of the tomato
sauce after they have cooked together for a few minutes. You must
increase the quantity of beef if it is to be eaten as a main course.

153

them quickly on all sides. Remove them from the pan
and set aside.
2. In the same pan, combine the tomatoes, garlic,
capers, parsley, salt and pepper, and cook over
moderately high heat for about 10 minutes, or until the
oil partly separates from the tomatoes.
3. Meanwhile cook and drain the spaghetti and dress
it with the rest of the oil. Return the meat to the frying
pan and warm it gently in the sauce. Pour the sauce
over the pasta, and serve.

Variations:

I. Add 3 or 4 anchovy fillets which have been
pounded to a thick paste in a mortar to the sauce
together with the tomatoes and other ingredients.

II. Add 2 ounces (60 gr.) stoned black olives to the
tomato mixture.

Penne with fresh mushrooms and tomatoes
Penne alla cacciatora

For 4 persons
12 ounces (350 gr.) penne or rigatoni
8 ounces (250 gr.) fresh mushrooms, the large kind, sliced
1 small onion, chopped
1 carrot, cut into matchsticks
*8 ounces (250 gr.) fresh tomatoes, peeled, or canned plum
tomatoes*
⅔ cup dry white wine
1 tablespoon parsley, chopped
3 tablespoons olive oil
freshly grated Parmesan cheese
salt and freshly ground black pepper

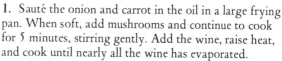

1. Sauté the onion and carrot in the oil in a large frying
pan. When soft, add mushrooms and continue to cook
for 5 minutes, stirring gently. Add the wine, raise heat,
and cook until nearly all the wine has evaporated.
2. Add the tomatoes (if you are using canned tomatoes
discard the juice) and the parsley. Mix carefully and
adjust seasoning. Cover, and simmer over low heat for
about 45 minutes, stirring occasionally.
3. Cook and drain the *penne.* Gently add them to the
vegetables. Add some freshly grated cheese, and mix
thoroughly over low heat for 1 minute. Turn into a hot
serving dish, and serve handing around a bowl of
Parmesan on the side.

This is an ideal way of using left-over chicken and the result is simply delicious and quite unusual.

For 4 to 6 persons
1 pound (500 gr.) ziti or large penne
8 ounces (250 gr.) boned cooked chicken, cut into small
    strips
4 tablespoons (60 gr.) butter
½ cup heavy (double) cream
2 teaspoons curry powder (or more if desired)
¼ cup dry white wine, or 3 tablespoons dry sherry, both good
    measures
2 tablespoons milk
1 tablespoon oil
¼ apple
1 tablespoon pine nuts (if not available, use almonds),
    chopped
1 tablespoon raisins (sultanas)
1 tablespoon brandy
2 bay leaves
salt

Large *penne* with curried chicken
Grandi Penne con Pollo al Curry

1. In a small saucepan combine the curry, butter, wine, oil, milk and bay leaves. Add salt and simmer for 15 minutes.
2. Drop the pasta into rapidly boiling salted water
3. Add brandy and cream to the curry sauce and boil for 1 minute. Then add the raisins, pine nuts, apple and chicken. Mix thoroughly, and keep warm over very low heat.
4. Drain the pasta, turn into a warm serving dish and pour over the sauce. Mix very thoroughly and serve at once. No cheese is needed.

For 4 to 5 persons
Tagliolini (thin tagliatelle) made with 2⅛ cups (300 gr.)
    all-purpose (plain) flour and 3 eggs (see page 102)
2 ounces (60 gr.) ham, diced
4 ounces (120 gr.) sweetbreads, diced
6 tablespoons (90 gr.) butter
½ cup dry white wine
½ cup heavy (double) cream
½ tablespoon fresh marjoram, chopped
½ tablespoon fresh thyme, chopped
pinch of nutmeg
salt and freshly ground black pepper
freshly grated Parmesan cheese

Tagliolini with sweetbreads and ham
Tagliolini con animelle e prosciutto cotto

1. Pour some warm water over the sweetbreads and soak for 10 minutes. Drain. In a saucepan, cover them with fresh water and bring to the boil. Boil for two minutes. Drain and refresh under cold water. If necessary, discard some of the skin. Dry them with paper towels.

2. Melt 4 tablespoons (60 gr.) of the butter in a saucepan. Add the herbs and ham and cook for 5 minutes. Add the sweetbreads and fry gently for 2 minutes. Pour over the wine, boil rapidly to reduce. Adjust seasoning and add nutmeg. Add the cream and cook, covered, over very low heat, for 10 minutes, stirring every now and then. If necessary add some warm water. The sauce should be of a coating consistency.

3. Cook the *tagliolini*, reserving ½ cup of the water and transfer to a warm dish. Toss with the remaining butter and then dress with the sauce and some of the water.

   Serve with a bowl of grated Parmesan on the side.

Noodle bows with kidneys
Farfalle con i rognoncini

For 4 persons
12 ounces (350 gr.) noodle bows
1 pound (500 gr.) lamb or veal kidneys
3 tablespoons vinegar
8 tablespoons (125 gr.) butter
2 tablespoons sherry
1 clove garlic, very finely chopped
3 tablespoons light (single) cream
2 tablespoons parsley, chopped
1 tablespoon all-purpose (plain) flour
salt and freshly ground black pepper

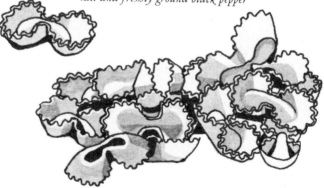

1. Split the kidneys in half lengthwise and using a pair of scissors, remove as much of the white skin and vessels as you can. Cut the kidneys into strips ½ inch

wide. Place them in a bowl, cover with cold water and
add the vinegar. Soak for about 1 hour. Drain and dry
with paper towels, and then flour the kidney pieces
lightly.
2. Drop the pasta into rapidly boiling salted water.
3. In a large frying pan, melt 6 tablespoons (90 gr.) of
the butter with the garlic. Add the kidneys and cook
over moderate heat, stirring continuously, for 1 minute.
Pour over the sherry, and boil rapidly for a further
minute. Reduce heat, add the cream, adjust seasoning,
and cook for about 3 minutes. Add 3 tablespoons of the
boiling pasta water to the sauce while it is cooking.
4. Drain the pasta and turn it into a warm serving
dish. Toss with the remaining butter, and cover with
the sauce. Sprinkle with parsley and serve.

This dish can be served as a main course, followed
by a salad.

Short pasta with meat bundles
Abissini con involtini

For 4 persons
10 ounces (300 gr.) short pasta
1 pound (500 gr.) pork fillets, sliced and flattened into thin
*   pieces approximately 3 × 2 inches (or smaller)*
4 ounces (125 gr.) smoked bacon
1 cup (100 gr.) Romano or Parmesan cheese, freshly grated
½ pound (250 gr.) fresh tomatoes, peeled, or canned plum
*   tomatoes*
1 small onion, chopped
1 tablespoon parsley, chopped
½ cup red wine
4 tablespoons olive oil (good corn oil would do)
Salt and freshly ground black pepper

1. Place a small slice of bacon, some parsley and some
cheese on the center of each slice of meat. Roll them up
into little bundles and fasten with a wooden toothpick.
2. Sauté the onion in the oil and, when transparent,
add the "bundles" and fry on all sides. Add the wine
and reduce by half over high heat.
3. Purée the tomatoes through a food mill and add to
the meat. Simmer, covered, for 15 minutes. Remove the
meat from the sauce and keep warm.
4. Drop the pasta into salted boiling water. Drain and
turn into a hot dish. Toss with the butter.
5. Pour the sauce over the pasta, mix thoroughly and
lay the "bundles" of meat on the top. Serve with the
remaining cheese on the side.

157

Penne with chicken sauce
Penne con salsa di pollo

This is a very economical recipe. The chicken, delicious cooked this way, is served as a separate course, hot or cold. The juices obtained from cooking the chicken are used to make the sauce for the pasta.

The making of this sauce requires a blender.

For 4 persons
12 ounces (350 gr.) **penne** or rigatoni
1 medium chicken
1 small onion, chopped
1 small carrot, chopped
1 small stick of celery, chopped
1 cup red or dry white wine
½ cup olive oil (or half olive oil and half good corn oil)
1 cup water
3 tablespoons (50 gr.) streaky smoked bacon, chopped
salt and freshly ground black pepper
2 tablespoons (30 gr.) butter
freshly grated Parmesan cheese

1. Put the chicken in an oval pan, into which it will just fit. Add all the vegetables, wine, water, oil and bacon. Cook, covered, over low heat until tender (approximately 1 − 1½ hours).
2. Uncover the saucepan and cook over high heat to reduce the liquid and brown the chicken. Remove the bird and carve from it about ½ cup of dark meat. Dice the meat.
3. Drop the pasta into salted boiling water.
4. In a blender, combine the juices in which the chicken has been cooked (you will need about 1½ cups) and the diced meat. If the sauce seems too runny, boil rapidly to reduce.
5. Drain the pasta. Turn it into a warm serving dish and toss with the butter. Cover with the sauce and serve with Parmesan on the side. If you wish to serve this dish as a main course, cover with a layer of sliced chicken.

Penne with veal and anchovy sauce
Penne con sugo di vitello e acciughe

This is another recipe which will provide 2 courses.

For 4 persons
12 ounces (350 gr.) **penne** or **lasagnette**
2 pounds (1000 gr.) very lean veal roast, boned and firmly tied (half a leg or top round)
10 tablespoons (150 gr.) butter
6 fillets of anchovy, chopped
the juice and grated rind of ½ a small lemon

$\frac{1}{2}$ *cup dry white wine*
1 cup stock or water
2 tablespoons parsley, chopped
1 clove garlic
1 tablespoon all-purpose (plain) flour
salt and freshly ground black pepper
freshly grated Parmesan cheese

1. In a heavy-bottomed casserole big enough to hold
the veal roast comfortably, melt 8 tablespoons (125
gr.) of the butter with the garlic clove. Add the
chopped anchovy fillets, and fry them in the butter,
mashing them up with a fork.
2. Add the veal to the casserole, and brown it quickly
on all sides. Remove the garlic. Add the lemon juice
and rind and salt and pepper.
3. Add the wine, and boil rapidly until it is reduced by
about half. Add the stock, cover, and simmer for
approximately $1\frac{1}{2}$ hours.
4. Remove the meat. You may serve it as a second
course, or cold at another meal.
5. Add flour to the pan juices, and mix it thoroughly,
away from the heat, scraping up all the coagulated
lumps. Add the parsley, and return the pan to the heat.
Cook for 5 minutes, stirring constantly.
6. While the sauce is cooking, cook and drain the
pasta. Turn it into a hot dish and toss with the
remaining butter. Pour over the sauce and serve with
the grated Parmesan on the side.

Like "*Penne* with chicken sauce," the meat is set
aside and eaten at another meal.

For 4 persons
12 ounces (350 gr.) macaroni
1 pheasant
8 tablespoons (120 gr.) butter
4 slices of streaky bacon
1 medium sized onion, chopped
1 stick of celery, chopped
3 egg yolks
1 cup red wine
a pinch of nutmeg
salt and freshly ground black pepper
$\frac{1}{2}$ *cup brandy*
2 tablespoons heavy (double) cream
freshly grated Parmesan cheese

Macaroni with pheasant sauce
Maccheroncini con salsa di fagiano

159

1. In a saucepan into which the pheasant will just fit, melt half the butter with two slices of the bacon. Add the bird and brown lightly on all sides. Add the brandy and boil very rapidly for about 1 minute. Add salt and pepper. Lower heat, and simmer, covered, for approximately 45 minutes, turning the pheasant occasionally.

2. Remove the bird, carve and set aside the breast and the legs. These can be used for another meal. Bone the rest of the pheasant and pound the meat.

3. Sauté the onion and celery in the rest of the butter. Chop the remaining 2 slices of bacon, add and cook for 10 minutes. Add the pheasant meat, the nutmeg and the seasoning and mix well. Pour in the wine and boil rapidly to reduce the liquids. If the sauce appears too dry, add a little stock. Simmer, covered, for 10 minutes.

4. Drop the pasta into rapidly boiling salted water.

5. 5 minutes before the pasta is done, remove the meat sauce from the heat, and add the egg yolks one at a time, beating hard after each addition. Add the cream and mix well.

6. Drain the macaroni. Turn into a hot serving dish, cover with the sauce. Mix well and serve with a bowl of grated Parmesan on the side.

Macaroni with sausages
Gomiti con la salsiccia

For 4 persons
12 ounces (350 gr.) macaroni or other short pasta
2 ounces (60 gr.) good lard or meat dripping
8 ounces (250 gr.) onion, finely chopped
4 ounces (125 gr.) sausages (Italian or Toulouse) cut into thin rounds
1 pound (500 gr.) fresh tomatoes, peeled, or canned plum tomatoes
½ small hot red pepper, crumbled
salt
freshly grated Parmesan cheese

1. Gently sauté the onion in the lard or meat dripping. When it becomes transparent, mush it up as much as possible with a wooden spoon. Add the sausage slices and cook for 5 minutes, making sure that the rounds stay whole.

2. Add the tomatoes, salt, and hot pepper to taste, and boil for 10 minutes or until the fat separates from the rest of the sauce.

3. Cook and drain the macaroni, pour into a hot dish,

and cover with the sauce. Serve immediately with the cheese in a separate bowl.

The juices of a pot roasted piece of beef are often used in Italy to create delicious pasta sauces.

For 4 persons
12 ounces (350 gr.) macaroni
1 pound (500 gr.) chuck steak, in a piece
1 large onion, finely chopped
1 carrot, chopped
1 stick of celery, chopped
6 tablespoons (90 gr.) butter
2 slices streaky, unsmoked bacon, cut into very thin strips
½ cup red wine (optional)
water
salt and freshly ground black pepper
freshly grated Parmesan cheese

Macaroni with sauce made from pot roast juices
Maccheroni al sugo di arrosto

1. In a saucepan into which the meat will just fit, sauté the bacon in the butter. Add the onion, carrot, and celery and sauté for 5 minutes. Add the meat and brown on all sides over moderately high heat. Pour over the wine, and boil rapidly to reduce the liquid. Add enough warm water to barely cover the meat. Adjust seasoning and simmer, covered, over very low heat for 3 to 4 hours, adding more water if the juice reduces too much. To make a good meat juice, you should pot roast the beef on the top of the stove for as long as possible.
2. Ten minutes before the meat is cooked (the juice should be brown, rich and thick in consistency) drop the pasta into rapidly boiling salted water.
3. Drain the pasta and turn it into a warmed serving bowl. Dress it with the meat juices. Mix and serve with a bowl of Parmesan cheese on the side.
    The meat is delicious and tender when cooked in this way. Serve it hot as a second course, or use it to make meat balls.

Cold pasta dishes

These are all modern dishes and are not at all a part of the traditional way of serving pasta. The thought of eating cold pasta would horrify any Italian peasant. However these dishes are quite delicious and make an easy and unusual summer luncheon course.

The pasta should be served tepid rather than cold or else it will become too gluey. The pasta is cooked in advance, tossed in olive oil and allowed to cool. Just before serving it is coated with a salad dressing, and I found the results delicious whichever of my favorite dressings I used.

Noodle bows with cold turkey
Farfalle con tacchino all'insalata

This is an excellent way to finish off the remains of the Christmas turkey. It is an unusual recipe, perfect for a cold lunch, to be served with a tossed green salad.

For 4 persons
10 ounces (300 gr.) noodle bows
1½ cups (250 gr.) cold turkey meat, diced
5 tablespoons olive oil
1 tablespoon wine vinegar
2 tablespoons capers
2 tablespoons cocktail pickles (gherkins), sliced
1 tablespoon pickled red pepper (paprika), cut into matchsticks
2 tablespoons parsley, chopped
salt and freshly ground black pepper
a few drops of Tabasco and Worcestershire sauces to taste

1. Cook and drain the pasta. Turn it into a large mixing bowl, toss with 2 tablespoons of the olive oil, and leave to cool.
2. Combine the turkey meat with the pickles and red pepper. Add the parsley, vinegar, Tabasco, Worcestershire sauce, and the rest of the oil and mix to a paste.
3. Combine the turkey mixture with the pasta, and serve cold.

Penne with mayonnaise
Penne con la mayonnaise

For 4 persons
10 ounces (300 gr.) penne or macaroni
2 tablespoons olive oil
3 tablespoons mayonnaise, preferably homemade, but a good commercial variety will do

1 tablespoon heavy (double) cream
7 fillets of anchovy, chopped
3 tablespoons fresh parsley, finely chopped
1 clove garlic, very finely chopped
3 hard boiled eggs
salt and freshly ground black pepper

1. Cook and drain the pasta. Refresh for two seconds under cold running water. Toss with the oil and set aside.
2. In a bowl, mix the garlic, mayonnaise, cream, anchovy and parsley to a smooth paste.
3. When the pasta is cool, or after 15 minutes, dress it with this paste. Mix well and adjust seasoning.
4. Pass the hard boiled eggs through the medium setting of a food mill, and sprinkle over the top of the pasta.

Variation:

Omit the hard boiled eggs, and decorate the top with 2 anchovy fillets cut into strips, and $\frac{1}{4}$ pound black olives.

Cold elbow macaroni with anchovies and sweet pepper
Chifferini all'insalata

For 4 persons
6 fillets of anchovy, pounded to a paste
12 ounces (350 gr.) elbow macaroni or other short pasta
8 ounces (250 gr.) fresh tomatoes, peeled, seeded, and cut into thin strips
1 clove garlic, crushed
2 drops Tabasco
$\frac{1}{2}$ teaspoon Worcestershire sauce
1 yellow or red pepper
5 tablespoons olive oil
2 tablespoons fresh basil or parsley
salt

1. Put the pepper under the broiler (grill) and cook it until the outer skin is black and blistered. Turn and repeat until the skin is charred on all sides. Quarter and peel the pepper carefully, discarding the seeds. Cut it into thin strips.
2. In a large bowl, combine the oil, anchovy paste, garlic, pepper, tomato strips, sauces and salt.
3. Drop the pasta into rapidly boiling salted water. Drain when *al dente,* and turn it into the bowl with the other ingredients. Mix thoroughly. Leave the pasta to cool for about 1 hour. Just before serving, sprinkle with the torn leaves of basil or chopped parsley.

Pasticci

Pasticci are dishes made with different kinds of pasta (usually short) and other ingredients and sauces. The distinguishing characteristic of these dishes is that all the ingredients are prepared separately and then are united for a final baking in the oven. The most familiar types of pasticci are baked lasagne and macaroni cheese. Very often they are topped with a Béchamel sauce or a mixture of eggs and cheese.

The pasticci are among the oldest pasta dishes. They were frequently served at elegant dinners in the eighteenth century and at that time they were usually known as *timballi* or *timpani*. Nowadays the word *timballo* is normally used to describe a pasticcio which is baked in a pastry shell.

The pasticci are substantial and nourishing dishes and they are particularly suitable for buffet parties since they look beautiful and are easy to eat with just a fork. The other advantage about them is that they can be prepared and assembled in advance, even the day before. In most cases it is advisable not to add the topping (e.g. Béchamel) until just before baking. They can also be frozen when completely finished. However I cannot recommend freezing homemade or store-bought pasta, as it would lose its fresh taste.

As a general rule the pasta in the pasticci is cooked twice: first boiled in water, and then baked in the oven. For this reason it is imperative that the pasta be *undercooked* in the water. Dry pasta should be removed from the boiling water at least 5 minutes before the recommended cooking time. Homemade fresh pasta should be lifted from the water just 20 seconds after the water returns to the boil.

Edmea Ordinanzi, winner of the 1972 Best Cook in Europe Competition, holding her winning entry, **Cappelletti alla Certosa di Pavia,** *Little pastry "hats" stuffed with meat.*

In December 1972 *The Sunday Times Magazine* and the Gas Council of
Great Britain held a competition for the Best Cook in Europe. The winner was
Miss Edmea Ordinanzi, who took the prize of £1000 from the English and
even the French competitors.

Miss Ordinanzi, a delightfully plump middle-aged woman set smilingly to
work on this fabulous dish. It is not something you can concoct in half an hour,
but what delicious food does not require time, love and patience? Here is the
recipe for you to use when you have an afternoon to dedicate to the demanding
and discerning palates of your family or friends.

If you have already mastered the method of making your own egg pasta, and
if you follow the steps carefully, your *timballo* is bound to be a winner too.

Little pastry "hats"
stuffed with meat
Cappelletti alla Certosa
di Pavia

To serve a large family

*1¼ lb. plain flour; 5 eggs and 1 egg yolk; 2 teaspoons salt;
6 oz. veal; 6 oz. pork loin; 4 oz. raw ham; about 2 oz.
Bologna sausage; salt; rosemary; 8 oz. Parmesan cheese, in
one piece; ½ pint double cream; 2 tablespoons breadcrumbs,
soaked in water and squeezed dry; 2 lb. chicken gizzards; 1
carrot; 1 onion, medium-sized; 1 small piece of celery; ¼
pint fresh tomato sauce; 1¼ pints meat stock; ½ pint olive
oil; 1 lb. butter; about ⅛ pint white wine, preferably Soave;
about ¼ pint red wine, preferably Chianti; nutmeg or cloves
to taste.*

For the pastry case: *6 oz. butter; 6 oz. flour sifted with
pinch of salt; cold water; beaten egg yolk to glaze.*

First make the stuffing for the *cappelletti.* Season the
veal and the pork with salt and a little powdered
rosemary. Brown them all over in 4 oz. of the butter
and ⅓ of the olive oil. Then pour in the white wine
and ¼ pint of the stock and simmer gently, covered, till
cooked.

Put the meat through the mincer with the ham and
the Bologna sausage. Stir in a lightly beaten egg yolk
into the minced meat, blend in well. Stir in 6 oz. of
grated Parmesan cheese and the breadcrumbs. Blend
smoothly together, and season if necessary, and leave to
cool.

Now make the pasta dough with the rest of the flour
and the 4 eggs, lightly beaten; knead for 25 minutes
until you have a soft, elastic dough. Let it rest for about
15 minutes. Then roll out very thinly and cut into small
pieces about 2 inches square. Put a little stuffing on
each one and fold it into the shape of a little hat.

(It takes about an hour to make the stuffing and 2
hours to finish making the *cappelletti* by hand.)

Now start on the chicken "sauce." Melt 6 oz. of
butter with the rest of the olive oil and cook the cleaned

and minced chicken gizzards with the finely chopped onion, celery and carrot, till all is soft and browned. When nicely browned, pour in the red wine and let it bubble until it has almost completely evaporated. Add the tomato sauce. (Preferably make this yourself with fresh tomatoes. If you are using concentrated tomato purée, dilute it with enough water to make it up to $\frac{1}{4}$ pint.) Stir it well in and pour in the rest of the stock. This "sauce" should be gently simmered, covered, for three hours.

When it is nearly ready, cook the *cappelletti* in plenty of boiling, salted water in a large saucepan; they will take only 4 to 5 minutes. When they are cooked, drain them well and stir them gently into the "sauce," together with the rest of the grated Parmesan cheese and the slightly warmed cream.

Finally, prepare the pastry case with flaky pastry made in the usual way, and rolled out very thinly. Use it to line a cake tin, 12 in. in diameter and $4\frac{1}{2}$ in. deep. Put the *cappelletti* and their sauce into the prepared tin and cover the dish with the rest of the pastry. Brush the top with egg yolk, beaten up with a few drops of cold water, and decorate with pastry flowers if you wish. Bake in a moderate oven, Gas Mark 4 [350°F], for about an hour until crisp, cooked through and golden.

Pasticcio of macaroni with tomatoes and mozzarella
Pasticcio di maccheroni alla Pugliese

for 4 to 6 persons
12 ounces (350 gr.) elbow macaroni
a Neapolitan tomato sauce made with 1½ pounds tomatoes (see page 112)
½ cup olive oil
4 ounces (125 gr.) Italian mozzarella cheese, thinly sliced
1 cup (100 gr.) Parmesan cheese, freshly grated
½ cup soft white breadcrumbs
½ cup fresh parsley, coarsely chopped
9 or 10 fresh basil leaves, torn (if available)
2 tablespoons dried oregano
a pinch of chili powder
salt and freshly ground black pepper

1. Half cook the pasta in rapidly boiling salted water. Drain.
2. Preheat oven to 350°F (Gas Mark 4).
3. Pour $\frac{1}{3}$ of the pasta into a buttered oven dish. Cover with $\frac{1}{3}$ each of the tomato sauce, the cheeses, the breadcrumbs and the herbs. Season, and sprinkle with 1 tablespoon of olive oil. Repeat for 2 more layers,

167

ending with a sprinkling of Parmesan and olive
oil. Cover the top with foil and bake for approximately
20 minutes. Remove foil, and bake for a further 10
minutes.

Red, white and green pasticcio
Pasticcio Tricolore

This is a patriotic dish; it is named after its
ingredients which match the colors of the Italian flag.

For 4 persons
12 ounces (350 gr.) elbow macaroni
1 pound (500 gr.) fresh tomatoes, peeled, or canned tomatoes
1 clove garlic, finely chopped
*4 ounces (125 gr.) Italian mozzarella, or Bel Paese, finely
    sliced*
1 small onion, chopped
8 tablespoons (120 gr.) butter
2 tablespoons fresh parsley, chopped
salt and freshly ground black pepper
1 dry hot red pepper, whole (optional)

1. Sauté the onion and garlic in 4 tablespoons of the
butter until soft and transparent. Add the tomatoes and
the red pepper (optional), and boil rapidly until the
sauce thickens (10 to 15 minutes). Remove the red
pepper and adjust seasoning.
2. Drop the pasta into rapidly boiling salted water and
cook until it is *al dente*. Drain.
3. While the pasta is cooking, purée the tomato sauce
in a food mill.
4. Turn on the broiler (grill).
5. Butter an oven dish, and turn the pasta into it. Toss
first with the remaining butter, and then with the
tomato sauce. Top with a layer of cheese. Put the dish
under the broiler until the cheese has melted, but remove
it before it turns brown. Sprinkle with parsley, and serve.

Pasticcio of tagliatelle with mushrooms and eggs
Pasticcio di tagliatelle alla boscaiola

This is a "woodcutter's" pasticcio. It calls for a less
rich *sfoglia* in which water is substituted for some of the
eggs. It is difficult to give the exact quantity of water;
the *sfoglia* should be elastic, smooth and compact like
that which is made with eggs, but it should not be
rolled out as thin.

For 6 persons
*Homemade pasta made with 3 cups (400 gr.) all-purpose
    (plain) flour, 2 eggs, and approximately ½ cup of
    water, and 1 teaspoon of salt (see page 102)*

6 ounces (190 gr.) mushrooms, chopped
3 eggs, separated
½ cup (50 gr.) Parmesan cheese, freshly grated
2 ounces (60 gr.) Gruyère cheese, finely sliced
2 ounces (60 gr.) Bel Paese cheese, finely sliced
2 or 3 slices white bread, with the crusts removed
8 tablespoons (125 gr.) butter
½ cup milk
½ cup heavy (double) cream
1 clove garlic
salt and freshly ground black pepper

1. Make the tagliatelle in the usual way, adding the water to the eggs before mixing in the flour, and let it dry.
2. Soak the bread in the milk.
3. In a frying pan, sauté the mushrooms and the garlic clove in 6 tablespoons (90 gr.) of the butter for 5 minutes. Remove the garlic.
4. In a mixing bowl, combine the egg yolks with the mushrooms. Squeeze the liquid out of the bread and add the bread to the mixture. Mash it with a fork.
5. Preheat the oven to 350°F (Gas Mark 4).
6. Beat the egg whites until stiff, and fold them into the mushroom mixture. Adjust seasoning.
7. Drop the pasta into rapidly boiling salted water, and drain it 1 minute after the water returns to the boil.
8. Into a large buttered oven dish, pour half of the pasta, all of the mushroom and egg mixture, and the sliced cheeses. Sprinkle with half of the Parmesan. Cover with the rest of the tagliatelle, pour over the cream, sprinkle with the remaining Parmesan, and dot with the rest of the butter.
9. Cover with foil and bake for approximately 20 minutes. Remove foil and brown the top quickly under the grill if you wish.

A very attractive and different dish, which is always successful. It takes about 1½ hours to prepare, but it is well worth the effort and the time.

Pasta roll with spinach filling
Raviolone di Spinaci

For 6 persons
Homemade pasta, made with 2 eggs and 1½ cups (200 gr.) all-purpose (plain) flour
2 pounds (1000 gr.) fresh spinach or two 10 ounce packages of frozen leaf spinach, thawed
1 clove garlic

169

6 tablespoons *(90 gr.) butter*
1 egg yolk
$\frac{1}{2}$ *cup (100 gr.) cottage cheese*
$\frac{1}{2}$ *cup (100 gr.) ricotta cheese*
$\frac{3}{4}$ *cup (75 gr.) Parmesan cheese, freshly grated*
pinch of nutmeg
Béchamel sauce made with $2\frac{1}{2}$ *cups milk (see page 113)*
salt and freshly ground black pepper

1. If you are using fresh spinach, discard any wilted leaves and the stems. Wash in a sink in several changes of cold water until the water is clear. Put in a saucepan without water, add 1 teaspoon of salt, cover and cook over a high heat for approximately 10 minutes, or until tender. If you are using frozen spinach, cook in a covered pan with 1 teaspoon of salt for 5 minutes. Drain the spinach, leave to cool and squeeze gently with your hands. Chop roughly and sauté gently for 5 minutes in a frying pan with 2 tablespoons (30 gr.) of butter and the garlic.

2. Transfer spinach to a bowl, having first removed the garlic. Add soft cheeses, nutmeg and egg yolk. Mix thoroughly and adjust seasoning.

3. Make the pasta as directed on page 102 and roll out thinly into one large rectangle. Spread the spinach filling over the pasta leaving a border of $\frac{1}{2}$ inch on three sides and 2 inches on one of the long sides. Roll up the pasta, beginning with the latter side. Wrap the roll tightly in a muslin cloth (or cheese cloth), tying the two ends securely with string, so that it looks like a large Christmas cracker.

4. Boil the salted water in a fish kettle or any other oval pan that will accommodate the roll. Put in the roll and simmer very gently, covered, for approximately 25 minutes. Lift the pasta roll carefully with the help of two spatulas or slotted spoons. Unwrap and set aside.

5. Preheat the oven to 350°F (Gas Mark 4).

6. Make the Béchamel and add the Parmesan.

7. Slice the pasta into slices $\frac{3}{4}$ inch thick. Put the slices into a large flat buttered oven dish. They must overlap slightly, but only form a single layer.

8. In a small saucepan melt the remaining butter and pour it over the slices. Cover them with the Béchamel.

Sprinkle with 1 tablespoon of breadcrumbs and bake in the top of the

oven until golden brown, approximately 30 minutes.
If necessary, put the dish under the broiler (grill) for a
few minutes.

Variation:

Do not make the Béchamel. Proceed with the first 7
steps, omitting step 5 (preheating the oven) as this
version is not baked. 8. Melt ¾ cup (150 gr.) of butter
in a pan until the foam has subsided. Pour over the
slices, sprinkle with ½ cup (50 gr.) of grated Parmesan
and hand around another ½ cup separately at the table.

For 4 persons
8 ounces (250 gr.) big pasta shells
4 ounces (125 gr.) ricotta or cottage cheese
1 egg
1 thick slice of white bread, without the crust, soaked in
*   milk and then squeezed out*
3 tablespoons parsley, chopped
a pinch of chili powder
a Béchamel sauce made with 2½ cups milk, well flavored
*   with nutmeg (see page 113)*
2 tablespoons (30 gr.) butter
½ cup (50 gr.) Parmesan or good Cheddar cheese, freshly
*   grated*
a little semolina
salt and freshly ground black pepper

**Big pasta shells stuffed
with ricotta**
*Conchiglioni ripieni di
ricotta*

1. Drop the shells into rapidly boiling salted water and
cook for 10 minutes. Drain well.
2. Preheat oven to 350°F (Gas Mark 4).
3. While the pasta is cooking, combine the ricotta in a
mixing bowl with the parsley, egg, half of the
Parmesan, chili powder, bread, salt and pepper. Mix
these ingredients very thoroughly.
4. Fill each shell with a little of the mixture and
sprinkle with semolina. (The semolina acts as a seal.)
Lay the shells in a large buttered oven dish. Pour over
the Béchamel and dot with butter. Sprinkle with the
remaining Parmesan and cover with foil. Bake for 30
minutes. Serve.

Variation:

Instead of Béchamel, cover the shells with a plain
tomato sauce (see page 111). Dot with 4 tablespoons
(60 gr.) butter and sprinkle with Parmesan. Bake as
above.

171

Pasticcio of *penne* **and**
eggplant
Pasticcio di penne e
melanzane

For 6 persons
12 ounces (350 gr.) **penne** *or elbow macaroni*
1 pound (500 gr.) eggplant (aubergines)
a plain tomato sauce (see page 111)
2 cloves garlic
2 ounces (60 gr.) mozzarella, or any soft cheese that melts
*   well (Jarlsberg, Gouda or Emmenthal)*
½ cup (50 gr.) Parmesan cheese or Farmhouse Cheddar
*   cheese, freshly grated*
4 tablespoons olive oil
2 tablespoons (30 gr.) butter
vegetable oil for frying
salt and freshly ground black pepper
a small handful of dry breadcrumbs

1. Slice the eggplant into thin rounds. (If the skin is
tough, you may wish to peel them first.) Sprinkle with
salt and place on a slanting board. Weigh them down
(I use a plate with a book on it), and leave to drain for
at least 1 hour. Pat dry with paper towels.
2. Prepare a tomato sauce (page 111).
3. Preheat oven to 350°F (Gas Mark 4).
4. A few slices at a time, fry the eggplant in 2 inches of
vegetable oil for about 5 minutes. When they are
golden brown, remove to a plate lined with paper
towels.
5. Drop the *penne* into rapidly boiling salted water,
and cook for 5 minutes less than the suggested time.
6. Butter a shallow oven dish, and sprinkle with dry
breadcrumbs. Drain the pasta, and toss, first with the
butter, and then with the tomato sauce. Cover the
bottom of the oven dish with a layer of *penne,* then add
a layer of eggplant and one of sliced mozzarella. Add a
few twists of freshly ground pepper from the mill.
Repeat these layers until the ingredients are used up,
ending with a layer of cheese. Sprinkle with grated
Parmesan or Cheddar, and dot with butter. Cover with
a piece of tin foil. Bake in a moderate oven for ½ hour,
but remove the foil after 15 minutes. Serve.

Variations:

I. Before baking, cover with a creamy Béchamel
sauce made with 2½ cups milk (see page 113) to which
the grated cheese has been added. This prevents the
pasta from becoming too dry, so do not use tin foil
during the baking. Instead of nutmeg, you may wish to
add garlic to the Béchamel. Do this by adding a clove

of garlic to the milk while it is being boiled, and then removing it. Or, for a stronger flavor, finely chop or crush a clove of garlic (in a garlic press), and add it to the butter and flour when you make the Béchamel.

II. Use lasagne instead of *penne* (see page 183 for cooking instructions). In this case, starting from the bottom, the layers would be: lasagne, eggplant, tomato sauce, cheese, ending with the grated cheese or the Béchamel.

Pasticcio of spaghetti and sardines

Pasticcio di spaghetti e sarde

Unlike the other pasticci in this section, this dish is not recommended for a buffet party as it is rather difficult to eat spaghetti standing up or sitting with the plate on one's lap.

For 5 to 6 persons
12 ounces (350 gr.) spaghetti
1 pound (500 gr.) fresh sardines
3 fillets of anchovy, cut into small pieces
8 ounces (250 gr.) fresh tomatoes, peeled, or canned plum
*   tomatoes*
1 clove garlic, finely chopped
5 tablespoons olive oil
1 tablespoon capers
2 tablespoons parsley, chopped
a small handful of dry breadcrumbs
1 tablespoon (15 gr.) butter
salt and freshly ground black pepper

1. Drop the spaghetti into rapidly boiling salted water. Drain it when very *al dente* and toss with 1 tablespoon of olive oil. Mix and set aside.
2. Cut the heads off the sardines and remove the bones. Wash, sprinkle lightly with salt, and set aside to drain.
3. Preheat oven to 350°F (Gas Mark 4).
4. Heat the remaining oil, and sauté the garlic quickly in it. Add the tomatoes (if canned tomatoes are used, discard some of the juice) and the sardines, and cook very gently for about 10 minutes, taking care to keep the fish whole. Adjust seasoning.
5. Butter a large, shallow oven dish. Cover the bottom with half of the spaghetti. Pour over the sardine sauce, and sprinkle with the anchovy pieces, the capers and the parsley. Cover with the rest of the spaghetti, sprinkle the top with breadcrumbs, and dot with the butter. Bake in a moderate oven for 20 minutes.

Pasticcio of short pasta and chicken

Pasticcio di penne e pollo

For 4 persons

10 ounces (300 gr.) **penne** *or elbow macaroni*
3 chicken legs (drumstick and thigh)
½ cup (50 gr.) bacon or ham (unsmoked bacon is best)
6 tablespoons (90 gr.) butter
3 tablespoons olive oil (good vegetable oil would do)
½ onion, chopped
1 small carrot, chopped
1 celery stick, chopped
½ cup dry white wine
*1 cup (100 gr.) chicken livers, chopped, from which any
     greenish spots and particles of fat have been removed*
1 cup (100 gr.) mushrooms, sliced
*a Béchamel sauce made with 2½ cups milk and a pinch of
     nutmeg (see page 113)*
*1 cup (100 gr.) Parmesan cheese, or Cheddar, freshly
grated*
salt and freshly ground black pepper

1. Heat the oil and butter in a heavy-bottomed frying pan large enough to hold the chicken pieces comfortably. Add the seasoned chicken legs and brown them on all sides. Reduce heat and cook gently for about 10 minutes, until the juices are released from the bones. Remove to a side dish, and cool.
2. In the same pan, combine the bacon, onion, carrot and celery. Cook for a few moments and add the mushrooms. Cook gently until soft. Add the chicken livers, and continue cooking for 5 minutes.
3. Meanwhile, bone the chicken legs, and cut the meat into cubes or small strips. Add the meat to the vegetables. Mix well.
4. Pour in the wine, and boil rapidly until the liquid is reduced by about half. Adjust seasoning. Cover, and simmer gently for 10 minutes.
5. Preheat oven to 350°F (Gas Mark 4).
6. Drop the pasta into rapidly boiling salted water, and stir it with a long fork. It will cook while the sauce is simmering. About 5 minutes before it is done, drain it and mix it with the sauce.

7. Butter an oven dish large enough to hold the pasta. Pour the pasta mixture into it. Cover with the Béchamel and sprinkle the top with half of the grated cheese. Bake for approximately 30 minutes. Serve with the rest of the cheese in a separate bowl.

For 4 persons

10 ounces (300 gr.) tagliatelle, store-bought or homemade, made with 2 eggs and 1½ cups (200 gr.) all-purpose (plain) flour (see page 102)
8 ounces (250 gr.) chicken livers, chopped, from which any fat particles and greenish spots have been removed
8 ounces (250 gr.) ham, diced
6 tablespoons (90 gr.) butter
4 ounces (125 gr.) cooked peas
2 eggs
½ cup light (single) cream
¾ cup (75 gr.) Parmesan cheese, freshly grated
a small handful of dry breadcrumbs
salt and freshly ground black pepper

Pasticcio of tagliatelle with chicken livers and ham

Pasticcio di tagliatelle con fegatini e prosciutto cotto

1. Sauté the onion in 4 tablespoons of the butter. Add the ham and cook for 2 to 3 minutes. Add the chicken livers and cook gently for a further 5 minutes. Add the peas, stir well and cook for 3 or 4 minutes. Adjust seasoning.
2. Preheat oven to 350°F (Gas Mark 4).
3. Slightly undercook the tagliatelle. If homemade pasta is being used, remember that it cooks in a few seconds once the water returns to the boil. Drain the tagliatelle.
4. Butter an oven dish and dust it with half of the breadcrumbs. Pour the tagliatelle into it, dress with 2 tablespoons of the butter, add the liver and ham sauce and mix thoroughly.
5. In a mixing bowl, combine the eggs with the grated cheese, cream and plenty of pepper. Pour this mixture over the pasta. Sprinkle with the remaining breadcrumbs and dot with butter. Bake in a moderate oven for about 30 minutes.

Variation:

Instead of peas, you may use 4 ounces of chopped mushrooms. Sauté these separately in 2 tablespoons (30 gr.) of butter and a squeeze of lemon juice, and add to the sauce after the livers.

175

Pasticcio of shells and chicken livers
Pasticcio di conchiglie e fegatini di pollo

For 4 persons
12 ounces (350 gr.) shell macaroni
8 ounces (250 gr.) chicken livers
1 onion, finely chopped
1 stick celery, finely chopped
1 small carrot, finely chopped
1 medium-sized leek, finely chopped; use only the white part
8 tablespoons (120 gr.) butter
1 tablespoon tomato paste
2 ounces (60 gr.) streaky bacon, chopped
salt and freshly ground black pepper
½ cup (50 gr.) Parmesan cheese, freshly grated (good Farmhouse Cheddar would do)
2 tablespoons water
3 to 4 leaves fresh sage, if available

1. Remove any greenish spots and bits of fat from the livers. Dry thoroughly and cut into small pieces.
2. Sauté the vegetables and the bacon in 6 tablespoons (90 gr.) of the butter until soft. Dilute the tomato paste in the water and add to the pan. Simmer, covered, for 30 minutes, stirring every now and then.
3. Preheat the oven to 350°F (Gas Mark 4).
4. Drop the pasta into rapidly boiling salted water and cook until very *al dente*.
5. Add the chicken livers to the vegetables and sauté for 2 to 3 minutes.
6. Butter an oven dish and add a layer of shells. Cover with some of the sauce and sprinkle with Parmesan. Repeat until all the ingredients are used up, finishing with the grated cheese.
7. Cover the dish with foil and bake for 15 minutes. Remove foil and continue to bake for a further 10 minutes.

Serve with some more grated cheese on the side if you wish.

Pasticcio of macaroni with meat and peas
Pasticcio di Garibaldi

This dish was reportedly created for the homesick Garibaldi when he was fighting in South America.

For 6 persons
12 ounces (350 gr.) macaroni, or other short pasta
8 ounces (250 gr.) fresh shelled peas
4 tablespoons (60 gr.) butter
*"Old-fashioned **ragù**" made with 8 ounces (250 gr.) chuck steak (see page 111)*

Béchamel sauce made with 2½ cups milk (see page 113)
    flavored with a pinch of nutmeg
½ cup (50 gr.) Parmesan cheese, freshly grated

1. Cook the peas, covered, in ½ cup of water, 2
tablespoons (15 gr.) of butter and 1 teaspoon of salt
until tender.
2. Preheat the oven to 350°F (Gas Mark 4).
3. Drop the pasta into rapidly boiling salted water.
Drain it when very *al dente.* Return it to the cooking
pot and toss with half the butter.
4. Add the peas to the *ragú.* Pour this sauce over the
pasta, mix thoroughly and then add half of the
Parmesan. Turn the pasta into a buttered oven dish.
Cover with the Béchamel, and the remaining cheese.
Dot with the remaining butter and bake for
approximately 30 minutes. You can hand around a bowl
of grated Parmesan on the side, if you wish.

A gourmet's pasticcio of lasagne
Pasticcio di Lasagne del Gourmet

For 4 persons
Homemade pasta made with 3 eggs and 2¼ cups (300 gr.)
    all-purpose (plain) flour or 10 ounces (300 gr.) dry
    lasagne
½ pound (250 gr.) ground lean beef
4 ounces (125 gr.) ham, chopped
1 egg
4 ounces (125 gr.) Italian mozzarella or Bel Paese, finely
    sliced
4 tablespoons (60 gr.) butter
1 cup plain tomato sauce (see page 111)
a Béchamel made with 2½ cups milk (see page 113)
2 tablespoons parsley, chopped
½ cup dry white wine
1 cup light (single) cream
½ cup meat stock or bouillon
½ clove garlic, finely chopped
salt and freshly ground black pepper

1. In a bowl, combine the meat, egg, parsley, garlic,
salt and pepper. Mix well and gently shape the mixture
into 10 to 12 small round balls. Roll them lightly in
flour. Fry the meat balls in the butter until they are
brown on all sides (approximately 5 minutes). Add the
wine and cook over high heat until the liquid has
reduced by half.
2. Make the Béchamel sauce. Remove from heat and
add the ham and cream to it.

177

3. If you are using homemade pasta, prepare the *sfoglia* (see page 102) and cut into rectangles about 5 by 3½ inches. Cook the pasta following the instructions for "Stuffed cannelloni" (see page 183). If you are using dry lasagne, follow the instructions on the box, but do not drop into the water more than 5 strips at a time. Do not overcook lasagne, or they will become mushy and tasteless.

4. Preheat the oven to 300°F (Gas Mark 3).

5. Butter an oven dish and cover with one layer of lasagne. Evenly distribute half the meat balls and half their juice over the pasta. Cover with 3 tablespoons of tomato sauce, one-third of the Béchamel and one-third of the cheese. Repeat for one more layer using the rest of the meat balls and tomato sauce, and one-third of the Béchamel and cheese. Cover with a final layer of lasagne, top with the remaining Béchamel and cheese.

6. Bake for 30 minutes. If necessary, put the dish under the broiler (grill) for a few minutes until the top is golden brown. Allow to settle for 10 minutes before serving.

Variation:

For a less heavy dish, omit the meat balls and the tomato sauce, and add to each layer ½ cup (50 gr.) of grated Parmesan and a pinch of nutmeg.

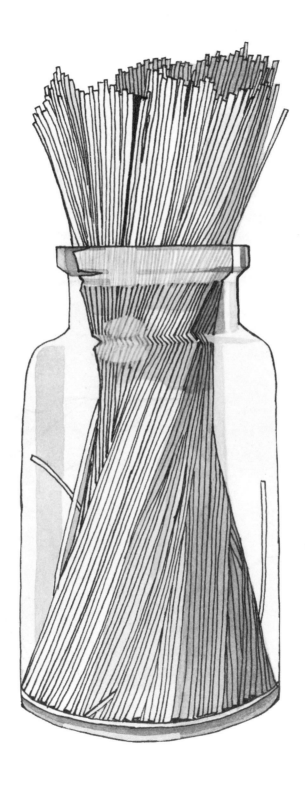

Regional recipes

All traditional Italian cooking is regional, and only in recent times have certain dishes become popular nationwide. Home cooking is still based on the availability of local products, and only fresh fruits and vegetables which are in season are used. For this reason traditional Italian cooking is always *genuino*: wholesome, unpretentious and fresh-tasting.

Each of the regional recipes in this section will help you to appreciate the diversity of local tastes and ingredients, and enable you to build up an overall picture of the world of Italian pasta.

Val d'Aosta

Pasticcio of ruffled lasagne with cheeses and mushrooms.
Pasticcio di Lasagnoni festonati alla Saint-Martin

A recipe that comes from the mountains of the Val d'Aosta where mushrooms are plentiful in the woods and the local cheeses are rich and sweet. Here I substitute more common cheeses for the original ones, which can only be found *in loco*. The ruffled lasagne used is a commercial kind, much easier and quicker to cook, because the pieces do not stick to each other.

For 6 to 8 persons
1 pound (500 gr.) ruffled lasagne
1 pound (500 gr.) fresh mushrooms, thinly sliced
1 cup heavy (double) cream
½ cup (60 gr.) ricotta or cottage cheese
4 ounces (120 gr.) Italian mozzarella, sliced
2 ounces (60 gr.) Fontina or Gruyère cheese, sliced
½ cup (50 gr.) Parmesan cheese, freshly grated
1 clove garlic, whole
12 tablespoons (180 gr.) butter
2 teaspoons fresh lemon juice
Salt and freshly ground black pepper

1. Sauté the mushrooms with the garlic clove in 4 tablespoons (60 gr.) of the butter, until just soft. Add the lemon juice, salt and pepper. Remove the garlic.
2. Preheat the oven to 350°F (Gas Mark 4).
3. Drop the pasta into salted boiling water and cook for about half of the recommended time. Drain.
4. Butter an oven dish. Cover the bottom of the dish with a layer of lasagne (use about one-quarter of the pasta). Cover with about one-third of the sliced cheeses and one-third of the mushrooms. Sprinkle with some Parmesan, salt and pepper and dot with 2 tablespoons (30 gr.) of the butter. Repeat this process until all ingredients are used up (3 layers), finishing with a layer of lasagne and the remaining butter and Parmesan. Pour the cream over the top. Cover with foil and bake for about 30 minutes. Remove the foil and run the dish under the broiler (grill) for a few minutes to brown the top. Leave the pasticcio to settle for 5 minutes before serving.

Piedmont

This is one of the few stuffed pasta recipes which did not originate in Emilia but in Piedmont. It is a dish that can be prepared in advance, apart from the last stage of covering the cannelloni with Béchamel sauce. The cannelloni can be stuffed with different mixtures. I give here two of the most common stuffings.

Both recipes can be made in advance up to step 3, and refrigerated or frozen.

Stuffed cannelloni
Cannelloni ripieni

For 6 persons
Homemade pasta made with 3 eggs and 2¼ cups (300 gr.)
    all-purpose (plain) flour (see page 102)
8 ounces (250 gr.) ground beef
4 ounces (125 gr.) luganega or any other kind of good
    Italian sausage
5 tablespoons olive oil (or good vegetable oil)
1 small onion, finely chopped
a sprig of rosemary
½ cup red or white wine, dry
2 tablespoons tomato paste, diluted in 2 tablespoons warm
    water
½ cup (50 gr.) Parmesan cheese freshly grated
salt and freshly ground black pepper
a pinch of crushed hot red chili pepper (optional)
3 tablespoons (45 gr.) butter
Béchamel sauce made with 2½ cups of milk and flavored
    with nutmeg (see page 113)

Cannelloni stuffed with meat
Cannelloni ripieni

1. Sauté the sprig of rosemary in the oil for 2 or 3 minutes. Discard the rosemary. Add the onion and the meat.
2. Remove the skin from the sausage and add to the meat. Brown on all sides. Adjust seasoning and add the hot red pepper. Add the wine and let it bubble a little until the liquid is reduced by two-thirds. Add the tomato paste, stir for 1 minute, reduce the heat and simmer for 1 hour.
3. In a mixing bowl, combine the meat sauce with the egg and half the cheese. Mix thoroughly to make a thick paste. Set aside.
4. Preheat oven to 350°F (Gas Mark 4).
5. Roll out the pasta dough into a thin *sfoglia* and cut it into rectangles of approximately 4 by 5 inches. Bring a large, shallow saucepan of water to the boil. Meanwhile

183

place a bowl of cold water near the stove. When the water is boiling add the salt and drop 5 or 6 rectangles of pasta into it. When the water has come back to the boil, wait about 3 minutes and then lift the pasta out with a large slotted spoon and plunge it immediately into the cold water. Lift it out and spread it on a dry cloth. Repeat this operation until all the pasta is cooked.
6. Butter a large, shallow oven dish. Spread 2 tablespoons of the meat mixture on each rectangle of pasta leaving $\frac{1}{2}$ inch border all around. Roll the strip up its narrow side. Lay it in the dish with the folded-over edge facing downwards. Proceed until all the meat or pasta is used up. You can pack cannelloni together tightly but they should all be in one layer.
7. Dot with 2 tablespoons (30 gr.) of butter and cover with the Béchamel. Sprinkle with the remaining Parmesan and dot again with 1 tablespoon (15 gr.) of butter. Bake in the oven for 20 minutes. Turn the oven off, and allow to settle for a further 10 minutes. If necessary, put under the broiler (grill) for a few minutes to brown the top.

Cannelloni stuffed with braised beef
Cannelloni ripieni di stracotto

For 6 persons
The minced or thinly chopped meat of 1 pound (500 gr.) of **stracotto** *(braised beef) (see page 195, "***Timballo** *of* **anolini**")
homemade pasta made with 3 eggs and 2¼ cups (300 gr.) all-purpose (plain) flour (see page 102)
2 eggs
2 tablespoons (30 gr.) butter
¾ cup (75 gr.) Parmesan cheese freshly grated
Béchamel sauce made with 2½ cups of milk and flavored with nutmeg (see page 113)

1. Mix the meat and eggs together very thoroughly. Add half of the cheese. Proceed from step 4 of the previous recipe.

Lentil and pasta soup
Pasta e lenticchie

Lentils are eaten in most parts of Italy. In Piedmont they are eaten at midnight on New Year's Eve, because they supposedly bring riches and wealth throughout the New Year.

For 6 persons
6 ounces (190 gr.) short pasta
8 ounces (250 gr.) dry brown lentils
½ cup olive oil

2 cloves garlic, chopped
6 cups stock or 2 to 4 stock cubes dissolved in 6 cups water
1 ham bone or 1 pig's trotter or 2 small pork chops
2 slices streaky bacon, chopped
3 tablespoons parsley, chopped
salt and freshly ground black pepper

1. Soak the lentils in water overnight. Drain, and rinse in cold water.
2. Put the lentils, pork, stock, and a little salt into a fairly large heavy-bottomed saucepan. Cover tightly and bring rapidly to the boil. Lower heat and simmer for about 2 hours, or until the lentils are cooked.
3. Add to the soup the bacon, oil, parsley, garlic, and pepper. Boil for 10 minutes. Adjust seasoning. Add the pasta and boil gently until cooked. Turn off the heat and leave it to stand for 5 minutes before serving.

This soup is usually served without cheese but, if desired, a bowl of grated Parmesan could be served on the side. The soup can be made ahead of time up to the stage of adding the pasta.

Lombardy

Ravioli are made in northern and central Italy. This excellent recipe is a specialty of Milan.

The two first steps can be prepared in advance and refrigerated or frozen.

Ravioli Milanese style
Ravioli alla milanese

For 4 persons
Homemade pasta made with 3 eggs and $2\frac{1}{4}$ cups (300 gr.)
all-purpose (plain) flour (see page 102)
2 ounces (60 gr.) bacon, very finely chopped
8 ounces (250 gr.) chuck steak
1 egg
1 sprig of fresh rosemary
8 tablespoons (120 gr.) butter
$\frac{1}{2}$ cup (50 gr.) Parmesan cheese, freshly grated
a pinch of cinnamon
5 leaves of fresh sage
1 clove garlic (optional)
$\frac{1}{2}$ cup water
salt and freshly ground black pepper
egg yolk and water (optional)

185

1. In a saucepan, heat half of the butter with the rosemary. Add the beef and brown it quickly on all sides over moderate heat. Reduce heat, add the water and correct seasoning. Cook, covered, over very low heat for about $1\frac{1}{2}$ hours, or until the meat is tender. You may have to add a bit more water during the cooking if the sauce becomes too dry. Remove the meat and chop it very finely, or grind it.

2. In a bowl, combine the chopped meat, bacon, 2 tablespoons of the Parmesan, the egg, cinnamon and some of the juices from the meat. Mix thoroughly.

3. Make the *sfoglia,* rolling it out as thin as possible. Proceed immediately to make the ravioli. Working quickly so as to prevent the pasta from drying out, lay out the *sfoglia* in front of you. With a fluted pastry wheel cut a straight line along the far side of the *sfoglia.* Drop small teaspoonfuls of filling at $1\frac{1}{2}$ inch intervals onto the *sfoglia* in a straight line $2\frac{1}{2}$ inches from the cut edge. Fold the edge of the pasta toward you just far enough to enclose the lumps of filling. Using a fluted pastry wheel, cut this ridge of stuffed pasta away from the rest of the *sfoglia,* and then cut straight across between each lump of filling to form small squares, or ravioli. Repeat until one or the other of the ingredients runs out. If the edges do not stick well, either pinch them together lightly with moistened fingers, or paint the edges before folding them over, with a mixture of egg yolk and water.

4. Drop the ravioli into a large saucepan of rapidly boiling salted water. Cover the saucepan and bring the water quickly back to the boil. Uncover and cook for at least 5 minutes. The timing differs according to the size and thickness of the ravioli, but 10 minutes should be the maximum.

5. While the pasta is cooking, melt the remaining butter in a small saucepan. Add the sage leaves, the whole clove of garlic, and the remaining juices from the meat after first removing the sprig of rosemary. Stir for 1 minute, remove the garlic, and pour the butter sauce into a warm serving bowl. Add the Parmesan.

6. Drain the ravioli and turn them into the serving bowl. Toss them quickly in the butter sauce, and serve at once.

A recipe from the Val d'Ossola near the Swiss border. The pastures there are very rich and the cheeses excellent. Here I am listing cheeses that can be easily found in the United States and in England, and which are good substitutes for the original ones.

For 4 to 6 persons
12 ounces (350 gr.) rigatoni
8 tablespoons (125 gr.) butter
1½ cups (225 gr.) sliced cheese: preferably ⅓ cup each of
    mozzarella, Gruyère and Dutch cheese
1 cup (100 gr.) Parmesan cheese, freshly grated
Béchamel sauce made with 2½ cups of milk (see page 113)
pinch of nutmeg
salt and freshly ground black pepper
1 tablespoon dried breadcrumbs

1. Preheat the oven to 300°F (Gas Mark 2).
2. While the pasta is cooking, make the Béchamel.
3. Drain the pasta when very *al dente*, toss with 6 tablespoons (90 gr.) of the butter and sprinkle with the Parmesan. Transfer half of it into a buttered oven dish. Lay the cheese slices over the pasta and cover with the rest of the pasta.
4. Cover with the Béchamel sauce, dot with the rest of the butter and sprinkle lightly with some dry breadcrumbs.
5. Bake for ½ hour or until brown. If necessary put under the broiler (grill) for a few minutes to brown the top.

Baked rigatoni with four cheeses
Rigatoni gratinati ai quattro formaggi

Venetia

Venetia is a very fertile and rich region, where vegetables grow particularly well because of good rainfall all through the year. Buy small and hard zucchini (courgettes) for this recipe, which is as simple and easy as it is delicious.

For 4 persons
12 ounces (350 gr.) short pasta
1 pound (500 gr.) zucchini
6 tablespoons olive oil
1 clove garlic, very finely chopped
3 to 4 tablespoons parsley, chopped
salt and freshly ground black pepper

Pasta with zucchini (courgettes)
Pasta con le zucchine

187

1. Wash, dry and finely slice the zucchini into rounds.
2. In a large frying pan sauté the zucchini and garlic in the oil until soft, approximately 20 minutes, taking care to stir them often so they do not stick or get too brown. They should be of a pale golden color. Add salt.
3. Drop the pasta into rapidly boiling salted water and drain when very *al dente*. Turn it into the frying pan, sprinkle with the parsley and season with several twists of the pepper mill. Fry for 1 to 2 minutes and serve at once. In Venetia cheese is not served with this sauce, but, if you wish, you can serve a bowl of grated Parmesan on the side.

Pasta and dried bean soup
Pasta e fagioli

This is a very thick peasant soup. In Italy it is made with dried beans, or with fresh beans when they are in season. It is never made with canned beans. Practically every region in Italy has its own variation. The first recipe I have selected is from the region around Venice, the second from Naples, and they are both made with dried beans, because fresh beans of the right sort are difficult to find in the United States or in England.

In Naples the pasta used for this soup is *munnezzaglia*, a name given to pasta of different shapes all mixed together. An ingenious way to use up the remaining small quantities of different packets. Long pasta, such as *ziti*, is cut into short pieces, and mixed with short pasta.

For 4 to 5 persons
4 ounces (125 gr.) **ditalini** *or any short pasta*
6 ounces (180 gr.) dried beans: kidney, **toscanelli** *or cranberry*
7 cups (or more if necessary) beef stock or bouillon
4 tablespoons (60 gr.) pork fat or dripping
2 ounces (60 gr.) streaky bacon, unsmoked, or **pancetta,** *chopped*
1 clove garlic, chopped
1 stick celery, chopped
1 small onion, chopped
1 pound (500 gr.) fresh tomatoes, peeled, or canned plum tomatoes
3 tablespoons parsley, chopped
salt and freshly ground black pepper
freshly grated Parmesan cheese

1. Soak the beans overnight in cold water to cover. Rinse and drain.

2. Sauté the bacon in the fat for 1 minute. Add the onion, garlic and celery and sauté for a further 2 minutes. Add the beans and cover with the stock. Boil, covered, for about 1 hour over low heat.

3. Roughly chop the tomatoes and add to the soup. Adjust seasoning, but be careful not to add too much salt, as the beans absorb a great quantity of the water. Simmer, covered, until the beans are tender. The timing varies according to the kind of beans, but it generally takes 2 to 3 hours.

4. Scoop out about half of the beans and purée them through a food mill. Return this purée to the pot. Add the parsley and the pasta and boil, covered, until the pasta is cooked. If the beans have absorbed too much stock, add more boiling stock before adding the pasta. Leave the soup to rest for about 5 minutes before serving. Serve a bowl of grated Parmesan on the side.

Neapolitan variation:

Omit the onion and substitute $\frac{1}{2}$ cup olive oil for the butter and bacon, and water for the stock.

1. Put the water in the saucepan. Add the beans (previously soaked overnight), garlic, tomatoes, salt and a good quantity of the pepper. Simmer, covered, until the beans are tender.

2. Add the oil, parsley, a few leaves of fresh basil (if available), and the pasta and simmer, covered, until the pasta is cooked. If the beans have absorbed too much water, you may have to add more boiling water before adding the pasta. This version is also excellent cold.

No cheese is served.

Trentino

This dish originates from Austria, where pasta is always served with meat, as a main course.

Steps 1, 2 and 3 can be prepared in advance, and the sauce refrigerated or frozen.

Tagliatelle with veal stew
Tagliatelle alla tirolese

For 6 persons
12 ounces (350 gr.) tagliatelle, preferably homemade (see page 102)
2 pounds (1000 gr.) stewing veal, cubed
7 ounces (225 gr.) onion, coarsely chopped
1 pound (500 gr.) fresh tomatoes, peeled, or canned tomatoes

189

12 tablespoons (180 gr.) butter
1 cup dry white wine
10 fresh sage leaves
1 teaspoon tomato paste
1 teaspoon ground paprika
1 tablespoon all-purpose (plain) flour
salt and freshly ground black pepper

1. Remove any fat or gristle from the veal.
2. Sauté the onion in 8 tablespoons of the butter until transparent (approximately 5 minutes). Add the veal, sage, paprika and tomato paste. Adjust seasoning, mix well and cook over moderate heat for 3 to 4 minutes, stirring all the time. Add the wine, raise the heat, and cook until the liquid is reduced by about half.
3. Stirring constantly, sprinkle the flour over the meat, add the tomatoes, and bring back to the boil. Lower heat, cover, and simmer gently for approximately 1 hour. If the sauce seems to be too dry, add 3 or 4 tablespoons of hot water during the cooking.
4. When the sauce is almost ready, drop the pasta into rapidly boiling salted water. When it is cooked, drain and turn it into a warm serving dish. Dress with the remaining butter and mix in half of the meat sauce.
5. Serve with the rest of the stew on the side.

Venetia Julia

Tagliatelle with goulash Triestine style
Tagliatelle con goulash alla triestina

This goulash from Trieste is as full-flavored and appetising as its more famous cousin from Hungary. It is an easily made dish, perfect for the hostess-cook, as it is served as a main course, which, apart from the cooking of the tagliatelle, can all be prepared in advance.

For 4 persons
12 ounces (350 gr.) tagliatelle, preferably homemade (see page 102)
1½ pounds (750 gr.) fillet of pork, cut into thin slices
2 tablespoons ground paprika, or more according to taste
1 tablespoon all-purpose (plain) flour
2 large onions, finely sliced
2 large red peppers
2 large fresh tomatoes, peeled and roughly chopped
4 tablespoons (60 gr.) butter
4 tablespoons (60 gr.) good lard or pork fat

$\frac{1}{2}$ *cup red wine*
1 cup beef stock or bouillon
1 tablespoon tomato paste
1 teaspoon grated lemon rind
salt and freshly ground black pepper

1. Remove seeds and white segments from the peppers
and cut them into thin strips.
2. Put the onions in a saucepan, and gently fry them in
the lard and half the butter for 5 minutes. Add the
meat, and brown on all sides. Mix in the paprika, flour
and tomato paste, and fry for 2 minutes, stirring
constantly. Adjust seasoning, and add lemon rind.
3. Pour the wine over the meat and boil rapidly for 2
to 3 minutes. Add the tomatoes and peppers, fry for 1
minute and cover with the stock. Simmer, covered, for
approximately 1 hour, adding a little warm water
during the cooking, if necessary. The sauce should be
rather thick and velvety.
4. Cook and drain the tagliatelle. Turn it into a warm
serving dish and toss with the remaining butter. Spoon
over some of the sauce and serve immediately with the
goulash on the side.

Liguria

This beautiful green sauce is truly food for the gods.
Traditionally, in Liguria, a potato is always cooked
with the pasta when it is served *al Pesto*. However the
dish is as delicious without it, and is now more
commonly served this way. Although the sauce is
slightly finer when it is made with a mortar and pestle,
it can be made quickly and very successfully in the
blender. This sauce freezes perfectly, so it can be made
in quantity while basil is in season and brought out
during the rest of the year. When making the sauce for
the freezer, omit the cheese, and fold it in just before
serving.

Trenette with **pesto**
Trenette al Pesto

Mortar **pesto**

For 4 persons
*10 ounces (300 gr.) linguine, **trenette** or thin spaghetti or
12 ounces (350 gr.) if you wish to omit the potato*
1 medium potato, peeled (optional)
*the leaves from one large bunch of basil, approximately 1$\frac{1}{2}$
cups*
2 cloves garlic

1 tablespoon pine nuts
6 tablespoons olive oil
½ cup Parmesan cheese, freshly grated
1 tablespoon Romano cheese, freshly grated
1 tablespoon salt, preferably rock salt
freshly ground black pepper

1. In a large mortar, preferably marble, pound the basil leaves, pine nuts, garlic, salt and pepper together until they are the consistency of a thick paste.
2. With a wooden spoon, fold in the cheese, and then, very slowly, the oil. Let stand for at least 1 hour.
3. Cut the potato into small cubes and drop them into a large pan of rapidly boiling salted water. When the potato cubes are nearly done, after about 15 minutes, add the pasta and cook until it is *al dente.* Drain, reserving 2 tablespoons of the cooking water. Turn into a warm serving bowl.
4. Quickly add the water to the *pesto* sauce, mix thoroughly, and pour over the pasta and potato mixture. Serve at once.

Blender *pesto*   Use the same ingredients as for the previous recipe.

1. Combine the basil, oil, pine nuts, garlic and salt in a blender and mix at high speed until a smooth paste is formed. If you use big, stringy basil leaves they may get tangled in the blades, so be selective.
2. Transfer the paste to a bowl and fold in the grated cheese. The sauce will be very thick. Serve as above.

The following recipe is a more sophisticated version, and the result is a more delicate sauce.

1 cup basil leaves
2 ounces (60 gr.) pine nuts
½ cup olive oil
1 clove garlic, chopped
1 tablespoon yogurt
4 tablespoons (60 gr.) butter
1 tablespoon parsley, chopped
1 cup (100 gr.) Parmesan cheese, freshly grated
salt and freshly ground black pepper

1. In the blender combine pine nuts, garlic, basil leaves, 1 tablespoon of the butter, oil, 1 teaspoon salt (rock salt if available) and the parsley. Blend until completely smooth. Add the cheese and mix again for $\frac{1}{2}$ minute.

2. Cook and drain the pasta, reserving 3 to 4 tablespoons of the water in which it has cooked. Turn the pasta into a hot dish and toss it with the remaining butter.

3. Add the yogurt and the water to the *pesto* and pour this sauce over the *trenette.* Mix thoroughly and serve at once.

If you wish you can serve some more grated Parmesan on the side.

For 4 persons
*Homemade fettuccine made with 3 eggs and 2¼ cups (300 gr.) of all-purpose (plain) flour (see page 102) or 12 ounces (350 gr.) store-bought **fettuccine***
1 pound (500 gr.) ripe tomatoes, peeled
5 tablespoons olive oil
3 cloves garlic, crushed
5 to 6 leaves of fresh basil, torn into a few pieces (if not available parsley can be substituted)

Fettuccine **with fresh tomatoes**
Fettuccine alla marinara

1. Cut each tomato into about 6 pieces and discard the seeds.

2. In a large frying pan, heat the oil and when it is hot, but not smoking, add the garlic, fry for 1 minute and then add the tomatoes. Cook for a further 3 minutes. Do not overcook or the flavor will be lost.

3. Cook the *fettuccine* and drain when very *al dente.* Turn into the frying pan and fry over moderate heat for 2 minutes.

No cheese is needed for this sauce, and canned tomatoes are not suitable.

Variation:

Cook the *fettuccine* until *al dente,* turn into a warm serving bowl, toss with 1 tablespoon of olive oil and mix thoroughly. Cover with the tomato sauce.

Emilia-Romagna

Baked green lasagne
Lasagne verdi pasticciate
alla modenese

This is a Modenese variation of the classic dish of baked lasagne, the great specialty of Emilia-Romagna. It can be made with spinach pasta or egg pasta or with store-bought lasagne. However, I advise you to spare the time and effort and make your own pasta. The final result is undoubtedly worth the trouble. Remember that store-bought lasagne takes 10 to 15 minutes to cook, while fresh homemade lasagne takes only about 3 to 5 minutes. This dish is rich and nourishing; it should be followed only by some salad and fresh fruit.

This dish may be prepared up to step 4 in advance and refrigerated or frozen.

For 4 persons
Homemade spinach pasta made with 3 eggs and 2¼ cups
(300 gr.) all-purpose (plain) flour (see page 109)
4 ounces (125 gr.) lean pork, coarsely ground
4 ounces (125 gr.) lean beef, coarsely ground
*2 ounces (60 gr.) lean bacon, unsmoked, or **pancetta***
1 small carrot, finely chopped
½ onion, finely chopped
1 small stick of celery, finely chopped
1 clove garlic, finely chopped
3 ounces (90 gr.) mushrooms, chopped
⅓ cup red wine
4 ounces (125 gr.) plain tomato sauce (see page 111)
1 tablespoon all-purpose (plain) flour
2 tablespoons parsley, chopped
2 tablespoons thyme, chopped
2 tablespoons olive oil (or good vegetable oil)
4 tablespoons (60 gr.) butter
a thick Béchamel sauce made with 2 cups milk (see page
113) flavored with onion and nutmeg
salt and freshly ground black pepper
1 cup (100 gr.) Parmesan cheese, freshly grated

1. In a frying pan sauté the onion, carrot, celery and garlic in half the butter for 2 minutes.
2. In a separate saucepan fry the bacon in the oil for 2 minutes. Add the sautéed vegetables and mix together. Add the meat and mushrooms, and cook, over moderate heat, for 4 to 5 minutes. Pour over the wine, add the parsley and thyme, and adjust seasoning. Boil until the wine has almost completely evaporated.

3. Add the flour and stir rapidly, over low heat, for 2 minutes. Add the tomato sauce, and simmer gently, uncovered, for about 1 hour. If the sauce becomes too dry, add a little warm water.

4. Preheat the oven to 350°F (Gas Mark 4).

5. Cut and cook the lasagne (see recipe for "Stuffed cannelloni" on page 183). Cover the bottom of a buttered shallow oven dish with a layer of lasagne. Cover with a little *ragú* (meat sauce) and some grated Parmesan. Repeat these two layers until all ingredients are used up. Top with the Béchamel and the remaining Parmesan.

6. Melt the remaining butter, pour it over the lasagne and bake in the oven for approximately $\frac{1}{2}$ hour. The top should be golden. If necessary pass under the broiler (grill) for a few minutes.

This is quite a time consuming dish to make but the end result looks marvelous and tastes delicious.

This dish may be prepared up to step 5 in advance, and refrigerated or frozen.

Timballo of *anolini* stuffed with braised beef (*stracotto*)
Timballo di anolini alla Piacentina

For 8 persons

1 small piece of beef roast, preferably chuck, weighing approximately 12 ounces (350 gr.)
1 onion, chopped
1 carrot, chopped
1 small stalk of celery, cut into pieces
8 tablespoons (120 gr.) butter
1 cup dry red wine
1 cup meat stock or bouillon
1 tablespoon concentrated tomato paste
1 clove garlic, finely chopped
$\frac{3}{4}$ cup (75 gr.) soft fresh breadcrumbs
2 eggs
$\frac{1}{2}$ cup (50 gr.) Parmesan cheese, freshly grated
a pinch of nutmeg
a *sfoglia* made with $2\frac{1}{4}$ cups (300 gr.) all-purpose (plain) flour and 3 eggs (see page 102)
a sweet pastry made with $2\frac{1}{4}$ cups (300 gr.) all-purpose (plain) flour, $\frac{1}{2}$ cup (100 gr.) sugar, and 6 tablespoons (90 gr.) butter
salt and freshly ground black pepper
egg yolk and water

1. In a saucepan, combine half of the butter with the onion, carrot, celery and garlic. Cook until the

195

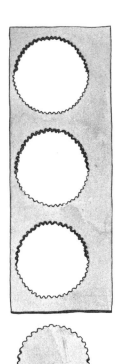

vegetables soften. Add the meat, raise the heat, and brown the meat quickly on all sides. Pour over the wine and boil rapidly until the liquid is almost completely evaporated. Add the tomato paste dissolved in the stock, lower the heat, and cook very gently, covered, for 3 to 4 hours. Add a little more stock or water if necessary. The juice should be thick.

2. In a bowl, soak the breadcrumbs and half the Parmesan in half the juice from the *stracotto* (the braised beef).

3. Mince or chop the meat very finely. Mix it with the eggs, breadcrumbs, cheese and nutmeg, and stir until they are well blended.

4. Prepare the *sfoglia* (see page 102) and cut it into rounds with a fluted cookie cutter (2 inches in diameter). To make the *anolini* put a teaspoon of the stuffing on each round, fold the dough over the stuffing in the shape of a crescent, and press down the edges with damp fingers.

5. Preheat oven to 300°F (Gas Mark 3 to 4).

6. Drop the *anolini* into a large saucepan of rapidly boiling salted water. They will cook in approximately 5 minutes. Lift them out of the water with a slotted spoon and put them into a bowl. Toss them with the remaining butter and cheese. Pour over the remaining pan juices from the *stracotto,* which have been gathered up with a bit of water.

7. Line a large, deep baking tin with some of the sweet short pastry. Pour into it the *anolini* without packing them down. If there are too many, refrigerate the remaining ones and use them another time. Cover the top with another round of pastry, and prick some holes in it with a fork. Brush the top with a little egg yolk mixed with 1 teaspoon of cold water and decorate with pastry shapes, if you wish. Bake in the oven for 50 to 60 minutes. Remove from the oven and let stand 10 minutes before serving with a bowl of grated Parmesan.

Tuscany

Pappardelle with hare
Pappardelle con la lepre

The Tuscans are Italy's keenest hunters. On the first day of the shooting season the whole region explodes. Pheasants, hares and even larks and thrushes become victims of this passion, the only good result of which is superb game recipes, like the following one for homemade pasta.

Pappardelle are very broad noodles (about 1 inch wide) with ruffled edges. They are cut with a fluted pastry wheel from a flat sheet of pasta which has been allowed to dry only briefly.

For 6 persons
*Homemade **pappardelle** made with 3 eggs and 2¼ cups*
  (300 gr.) all-purpose (plain) flour (see page 102)
the front legs of a hare
1 small onion, finely chopped
1 carrot, finely chopped
1 stick of celery, chopped
2 tablespoons parsley, chopped
2 teaspoons all-purpose (plain) flour
1 cup red wine
1 cup stock or water
1 or 2 cloves garlic, finely chopped
2 tablespoons olive oil (good corn oil would do)
6 tablespoons (90 gr.) butter
1 ounce (30 gr.) streaky bacon, chopped (preferably
  unsmoked)
2 tablespoons heavy (double) cream
a pinch of grated nutmeg
a small sprig of rosemary
salt and freshly ground black pepper

1. Sauté the bacon in the oil and 4 tablespoons (60 gr.) of the butter. Add the onion and cook for a few minutes, until it is transparent. Add the carrot, celery, garlic, and rosemary and sauté for a further 5 minutes.
2. Add the hare legs and brown them on all sides. Add flour, and brown, stirring rapidly. Add the wine, raise heat, and cook until the liquid has reduced by half. Add the cream and nutmeg. Mix well and adjust seasoning. Add ½ cup of water or stock. The sauce should be rather thick. Reduce heat, cover, and cook for a good hour, stirring occasionally and adding the remaining water or stock during the cooking.
3. Remove the hare legs from the pan. Bone them and cut the meat into small pieces. Return the meat to the sauce, and keep it hot.
4. Cook and drain the *pappardelle*. Toss them with the remaining butter, turn them into a hot serving dish, and cover with the sauce. Mix well, sprinkle with parsley, and serve.

In Tuscany this dish is served without cheese, but some Parmesan could be served on the side, if desired.

197

Broad beans and pasta soup

Minestra di fave

This is a traditional recipe for a Tuscan soup.

For 6 persons:
4 ounces (125 gr.) small macaroni
1 large onion, cut in rings
2 cloves garlic, chopped
1 pound (500 gr.) fresh shelled young broad beans, or
*   frozen or canned broad beans*
5 cups light chicken stock or 2 to 4 chicken bouillon cubes
*   dissolved in 5 cups of water*
5 tablespoons olive oil
2 tablespoons concentrated tomato paste
1 bay leaf
2 tablespoons ricotta or cottage cheese
salt and freshly ground black pepper

1. Sauté the onions and garlic in the oil for 5 minutes. Add the tomato paste and the bay leaf and fry for 1 minute. Add the broad beans, and fry for 2 minutes, stirring constantly. Cover with the stock and adjust seasoning, and cook for about 10 minutes.
2. When the broad beans are cooked, remove bay leaf, lift approximately half of the broad beans out of the pan with a slotted spoon and put them on a plate. Peel them. Also lift out as many onion rings as possible and add them to the peeled broad beans.
3. Purée the rest of the soup. Return it to the saucepan, add the pasta and boil gently until it is cooked. Add the peeled broad beans, the onion rings and ricotta. Stir over low heat for 1 minute. Serve. A bowl of grated Parmesan cheese can be served on the side, if desired.

Marches

Squid, *calamaroni,* is not very popular either in the United States or in England. It is in fact an excellent mollusc, much appreciated in fish loving countries like Italy, Spain and Japan. I include these two delicious pasta sauces, which come from Pesaro in the Marches on the Adriatic, but, in fact, are very similar to those served in Leighhorn on the Mediterranean coast.

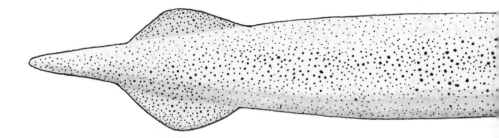

For 6 persons
12 ounces (350 gr.) spaghetti
1 pound (500 gr.) squid, preferably small
½ onion, finely chopped
½ pound (250 gr.) fresh tomatoes, peeled, or canned plum
   tomatoes
1 clove garlic, finely chopped
6 tablespoons olive oil
3 tablespoons parsley, chopped
½ cup red or dry white wine
Pinch of dry red chili pepper (optional)

Spaghetti with squid I
Spaghetti con le seppie

1. Clean the squid as follows: hold the sack in one
hand and with the other pull off the tentacles. As you
pull them, the internal organs should come out of the
sack. Reserve the tentacles and the sack and discard the
organs. Remove the bone from the sack and peel off as
much as you can of the skin under running water. Wash
thoroughly both sack and tentacles and dry with
kitchen towels. Cut the tentacles into small pieces and
the sack into thin strips.
2. Sauté the onion in 4 tablespoons of the oil until soft.
Press the onion against the sides of the pan with a
wooden spoon to release the juices. Add the tomatoes
and cook uncovered for 10 minutes over moderately
high heat.
3. Add the squid tentacles, and cook for 5 minutes.
Then add the sacks and cook for a further 5 minutes.
Pour in the wine and boil rapidly for 2 minutes. Adjust
seasoning and add the red pepper. Simmer gently until
the squid is tender, usually about 45 minutes depending
upon size.
4. About 10 minutes before the sauce is ready, drop
the spaghetti into boiling salted water.
5. At the same time add the parsley and the garlic to
the sauce. Stir occasionally during cooking, and if the
sauce becomes too dry add a little warm water.
6. Drain the spaghetti. Turn into a serving bowl, dress
with the rest of the oil and then cover with the sauce.
Mix thoroughly and serve.
   No cheese is needed.

Spaghetti with squid II

This variation calls for the ink from the ink bags of the squid, and has no tomatoes in it. It has a brilliant color and a delicious fishy taste.

For 5 to 6 persons
12 ounces (350 gr.) spaghetti
1 pound (500 gr.) squid, cleaned and prepared as for recipe
    I, but retaining 3 or 4 ink bags
1 small onion, finely chopped
2 cloves garlic
5 tablespoons olive oil
½ cup red wine
3 tablespoons parsley, chopped
salt and freshly ground black pepper

1. Proceed as for the preceding recipe, but omit the tomatoes, and add the ink squeezed from the ink bags before adding the wine.

Pappardelle with veal, anchovy fillets and tomato sauce
Pappardelle alla Maceratese

Pappardelle are a Tuscan speciality, but they are found also in the Marches, on the Eastern side of the Appenines.

They are broad noodles with ruffled edges (1 inch wide), cut with a fluted pastry wheel from a *sfoglia* which has been allowed to dry only briefly.

For 4 persons
Homemade pasta made with 3 eggs and 2¼ cups (300 gr.)
    all-purpose (plain) flour (see page 102)
6 ounces (180 gr.) lean veal, coarsely ground
8 ounces (250 gr.) plain tomato sauce (see page 111)
1 onion, chopped
1 celery stick, chopped
4 tablespoons (60 gr.) butter
*2 ounces (30 gr.) streaky bacon, unsmoked, or **pancetta**, cut*
    into small pieces
4 anchovy fillets, mashed with pestle and mortar
½ cup dry white wine
salt and freshly ground black pepper
freshly grated Parmesan cheese

1. In a saucepan gently fry the bacon in half of the butter for 1 to 2 minutes. Add the onion and celery and sauté for 5 minutes. Add the meat and brown quickly on all sides. Pour over the wine and reduce the liquid over high heat. Add the anchovy fillets and cook for 2 to 3 minutes.

2. Add the tomato sauce and simmer, covered, for approximately ½ hour, adding a little warm water if the sauce becomes too dry.

3. Cook and drain the *pappardelle.* Turn them into a warm serving bowl, toss with the remaining butter and serve at once, with the grated Parmesan on the side.

Umbria

This old-fashioned recipe comes from the mountains around Perugia, where bay trees grow wild. It has quite an unusual, delicious taste.

For 4 persons
12 ounces (350 gr.) thin spaghetti or **tagliolini**
14 ounces (420 gr.) fresh tomatoes, peeled, or canned
    tomatoes, roughly chopped
1 large onion, finely chopped
4 tablespoons olive oil
10 fresh bay leaves
¼ teaspoon cinnamon
salt and freshly ground black pepper

Thin spaghetti with tomatoes, bay leaves and cinnamon
Spaghettini alla moda di Umbertide

1. In a large frying pan sauté the onion in the oil until transparent. Add the tomatoes (if you are using canned tomatoes, discard half of the juice), the bay leaves, cinnamon, salt and a fair amount of pepper. Cook, uncovered, for 15 minutes, stirring every now and then.

2. Drop the pasta into rapidly boiling salted water. Drain it when very *al dente,* reserving 2 to 3 tablespoons of the water. Turn it into the frying pan, add the water from the cooking of the pasta and fry for 1 minute, stirring constantly. Serve at once. No cheese is served with this sauce.

Abruzzi

This is an old recipe from the mountainous region of Abruzzi where it is made with pork jowl, and, if you can get it, it is preferable. Salt pork is, however, a perfectly good substitute.

For 4 persons
12 ounces (350 gr.) **bucatini** *or* **mostacciolini**
1 cup (200 gr.) salt pork, cut into matchsticks

Bucatini with salt pork
Bucatini all'Amatriciana

201

2 tablespoons olive oil
1 pound (500 gr.) fresh tomatoes, peeled, or canned plum
    tomatoes with some of the juice discarded
1 (or 2, according to taste) hot red chili peppers, crumbled
2 tablespoons onion, finely chopped
⅔ cup (75 gr.) Romano cheese, freshly grated

1. Sauté the pork in the oil over medium heat until the fat is transparent, approximately 10 minutes. With a slotted spoon, remove meat to a side dish.
2. Add the onion, tomatoes and red pepper to the saucepan and sauté gently for 5 minutes.
3. Return the meat to the saucepan, and simmer for 15 minutes.
4. Drop the pasta into rapidly boiling salted water. Drain it, and turn it into a warm serving dish. Cover the pasta with the sauce and half the grated cheese. Serve immediately, serving the rest of the cheese in a bowl on the side.

Variation:

Substitute unsmoked bacon for the salt pork and increase the quantity of hot red pepper, according to taste. This version is known as *all' arrabbiata* – "angry bucatini," so called because the sauce is very hot.

Molise

**Homemade pasta with
hot lamb sauce**
Maccheroni alla chitarra

This is one of the oldest specialties of Abruzzi and Molise. The homemade pasta of this recipe is cut with the *chitarra* (guitar). A *sfoglia* the same size as the *chitarra* is laid on the *chitarra* itself. The *sfoglia* is then pressed through the strings with a rolling pin, thus producing long, oblong strips.

The following sauce is excellent with homemade *fettuccine* or thin spaghetti. In Molise the meat is served as a second course accompanied by some green vegetables, or at a different meal. You could serve it, however, with the pasta on the same dish.

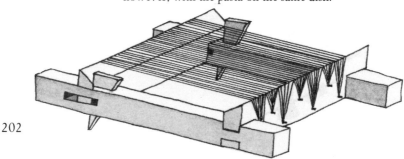

For 4 persons

Homemade **fettuccine** *made with 3 eggs and 2¼ cups (300*
gr.) all-purpose (plain) flour (see page 102)
2 pounds (1000 gr.) best end neck of lamb (ask your
butcher to chine it for you)
4 tablespoons (60 gr.) dripping
2 tablespoons olive oil or good vegetable oil
4 ounces (125 gr.) mushrooms, chopped
1 tablespoon all-purpose (plain) flour
2 tablespoons tomato paste
1 small onion, chopped
1 clove garlic, crushed
¼ cup red wine
3 tablespoons wine vinegar
¼ cup water
1 hot red chili pepper, crumbled
1 tablespoon parsley, chopped
1 tablespoon oregano
salt

1. Heat the dripping in a saucepan. When hot add the
meat, season with red pepper, garlic, oregano and salt,
and brown on all sides for 10 minutes. Lift out the
meat, and put on a dish to one side.
2. Add the oil to the saucepan, and heat. When it
begins to smoke add the mushrooms, and sauté for 5
minutes. Lift the mushrooms with a slotted spoon, and
put on the dish with the lamb.
3. Put the onion into the saucepan, sauté until golden,
pour over the wine and vinegar, and boil rapidly until
the liquid has nearly all evaporated.
4. Remove from heat, add the flour, and cook for 1
minute. Add the tomato paste, cook for a further 2
minutes, and cover with the water. Cook, uncovered,
over very low heat, for 15 minutes, adding more warm
water during the cooking if the sauce becomes too dry.
Stir occasionally.
5. Return the lamb and mushrooms to the saucepan,
and cook, covered, for 30 minutes, or until the lamb is
done.
6. Drop the pasta into rapidly boiling salted water.
7. Lift out the meat, and put aside.
8. Drain the pasta, leaving it dripping with the water
in which it was cooked, and turn into a warm serving
bowl.

Cover with the sauce, sprinkle with the parsley
and serve immediately.

Latium

Spaghetti with anchovy fillets and olives
Spaghetti alla Puttanesca

This very old recipe from Rome has its origins in the poor district of *Trastevere,* the traditional haunt of Roman prostitutes. Its name (a *puttana* is a prostitute) no doubt owes something to the fact that it is a hot sauce, very quickly made.

For 4 persons
12 ounces (350 gr.) spaghetti
8 ounces (250 gr.) fresh tomatoes, peeled
4 ounces (125 gr.) black olives, the large Greek kind, stoned and sliced
8 anchovy fillets, chopped
1 tablespoon capers
2 cloves garlic, finely sliced
1 tablespoon parsley, chopped
3 tablespoons olive oil
4 tablespoons (60 gr.) butter
½ hot red chili pepper, crumbled (or more, if desired)
salt

1. Discard the seeds from the fresh tomatoes, and cut them into thin strips.
2. Drop the spaghetti into rapidly boiling salted water.
3. In a large frying pan, combine the butter, oil, anchovies, garlic, red pepper and fry for 1 minute. Add the tomatoes, olives and capers, and cook for a couple of minutes. Adjust seasoning.
4. Drain the spaghetti when very *al dente,* and add to the frying pan together with the parsley. Fry for 1 minute, stirring constantly. Serve at once. No cheese is served with this sauce.

Pasta and chickpea soup
Pasta e ceci

This is a more modern version, still very old however, of the soup mentioned by Horace, as described on page 118.
This soup can be made ahead of time up to the stage of adding the pasta and then refrigerated or frozen.

For 6 persons
6 ounces (180 gr.) elbow macaroni or any kind of small short pasta
6 ounces (180 gr.) dried chickpeas
½ cup olive oil
2 cloves garlic, chopped

6 cups stock or water
1 bay leaf
salt and freshly ground black pepper

1. Soak the chickpeas in water overnight, changing the water once.
2. Drain the chickpeas and rinse them again in fresh water. Put them into a good-sized, heavy-bottomed saucepan, add the stock or water, bay leaf, garlic, oil, salt and pepper. Cover tightly and bring the soup rapidly to the boil. Lower heat and simmer for about 3 hours. Do not uncover the pan or the chickpeas will become hard and will not cook properly.
3. Add the pasta and adjust seasoning. When the pasta is cooked, allow the soup to settle for 5 minutes before serving. A bowl of freshly grated Parmesan can be served on the side, if desired.

Campania

Naples is the motherland of pasta. From the many sauces that come from this city and its surrounding countryside, I have chosen these three that are connected particularly with Naples and the sea.

Buy mussels in their shells, which must be tightly closed. Bottled mussels should not be used, as they flavor the sauce with vinegar.

Spaghetti with mussels and tomatoes
Spaghetti con cozze e sugo di pommodoro

For 4 persons
12 ounces (350 gr.) spaghetti or vermicelli
2 quarts (1000 gr.) mussels
1 pound (500 gr.) fresh tomatoes, peeled, or canned plum tomatoes
2 cloves garlic, finely chopped
2 tablespoons parsley, chopped
4 tablespoons olive oil
salt and freshly ground black pepper

1. To clean the mussels, put them in a sink and scrub them thoroughly with a hard brush, scraping off any barnacles with a knife. Place them in a colander and leave them under cold running water until they are clean.

2. When they are clean, place the mussels in a large pan. Cover it, and cook them over high heat until they open, turning them occasionally. Remove the meat from the shells and discard the shells. Strain the liquid that remains at the bottom of the pan through a cheese cloth and reduce it over high heat. You should have about 1 cup.

3. Heat the oil and garlic in a frying pan. Add the tomatoes (if you are using canned tomatoes, discard the juice) and boil, uncovered, over high heat for 5 minutes. Add $\frac{1}{2}$ cup of the mussel juice. Adjust seasoning.

4. Drop the pasta into rapidly boiling salted water to which you have added the remaining mussel juice.

5. Add the mussels to the tomato sauce and cook them gently for 5 minutes. Stir in the parsley.

6. Drain the pasta and turn it into a hot serving dish. Pour the sauce over it and mix well. No cheese is ever served with mollusc sauces.

Spaghetti with mussels
Spaghetti in bianco con le cozze

For 4 persons
12 ounces (350 gr.) spaghetti
2 quarts (1000 gr.) mussels
3 cloves garlic, finely chopped
3 tablespoons parsley, chopped
5 tablespoons olive oil
the grated rind of half a lemon
salt and freshly ground black pepper
$\frac{1}{2}$ tablespoon dry oregano (optional)

Prepare the mussels according to steps 1 and 2 of the preceding recipe.

3. Heat the oil with the garlic in a large frying pan. Add the strained and reduced liquid slowly, discarding the sediment that remains at the bottom of the bowl. Cook for 1 minute over high heat. Add the lemon rind, salt, pepper, oregano and parsley. Mix well. Add the mussels, and cook over moderate heat until they are hot, approximately 5 minutes.

4. Drop the pasta into rapidly boiling salted water and cook until it is *al dente*. Drain and turn it into a warm serving bowl. Pour the sauce over it and serve without cheese.

For 4 persons
12 ounces (350 gr.) thin spaghetti
2 dozen littleneck clams
14 ounces (450 gr.) fresh tomatoes, peeled, or canned
*   tomatoes, chopped*
2 cloves garlic, finely chopped
2 tablespoons parsley, chopped
4 tablespoons olive oil
salt and freshly ground black pepper

Thin spaghetti with clam and tomato sauce
Spaghettini con le vongole

1. Buy the tiniest clams you can find. Put them in a sink and scrub them thoroughly with a hard brush. Place them in a colander and leave them under cold running water until they are clean.
2. When they are clean, place the clams in a heavy-bottomed pan. Cover it and cook the clams over high heat until they open, turning them occasionally. Remove the clams from the shells and discard the shells. Unless the clams are exceptionally small, cut them in half. Strain the liquid that remains at the bottom of the pan through a muslin cloth.
3. Heat the oil, garlic and 1 tablespoon of parsley over moderately high heat. Add the strained liquid and reduce to about ½ cup over high heat. Add the tomatoes and cook, uncovered, for 15 minutes, over high heat. Adjust seasoning.
4. While the sauce is cooking, drop the pasta into rapidly boiling salted water.
5. Remove the sauce from the heat and add the clams. Then keep the sauce warm, but be sure not to let it boil.
6. Drain the thin spaghetti and turn it into a hot serving bowl. Pour the sauce over it, mix well and sprinkle the remaining parsley on the top.
   No cheese is needed with this dish.

Lucania

In Lucania the peppers are big and fat and of a brilliant red and yellow color. This recipe should be made with this kind of pepper in order to achieve the perfect combination of the sweetness of the vegetables and the hotness of the hot red pepper (chili). If you use green peppers, you will lose the sweet taste.

Spaghetti with grilled peppers
Spaghetti coi peperoni arrostiti

For 4 persons
12 ounces (350 gr.) spaghetti
4 large yellow or red peppers
2 cloves garlic
9 tablespoons olive oil
3 tablespoons parsley, chopped
½ hot red chili pepper, crumbled
salt

1. Put the peppers under the broiler (grill). Cook until the outer skin is black and broken. Turn and repeat until the skin is charred on all sides. Peel them carefully, using a small knife, if necessary. Wipe them with paper towels, but do not wash them or some of the taste will be lost. Cut each pepper into quarters, discard seeds and white segments and cut into small strips.
2. Drop the spaghetti into rapidly boiling salted water.
3. In a large frying pan sauté the garlic in the oil for 1 minute. Add the peppers and the hot red pepper and fry gently for a further 4 minutes. Correct seasoning.
4. Drain the spaghetti when very *al dente* and turn it into the frying pan. Sprinkle with the parsley and fry for 1 to 2 minutes.

No cheese is served with this sauce.

Calabria

Pasticcio of spaghetti and grilled peppers
Pasticcio di spaghetti e peperoni arrostiti

This recipe calls for the big, fat red and yellow peppers. Although green peppers could be used, the sweet taste would be lost.

For 4 persons
12 ounces (350 gr.) spaghetti
4 large yellow or red peppers
2 cloves garlic
8 tablespoons olive oil
3 tablespoons parsley, chopped
3 tablespoons soft breadcrumbs
3 ounces (100 gr.) black olives, stoned
1 tablespoon capers
salt and freshly ground black pepper

1. Put the peppers under the broiler (grill). Cook until the outer skin is black and broken on all sides. Peel very carefully, using a small knife if necessary. Wipe them with paper towels. Cut each pepper into quarters,

discard seeds and white segments and cut into small strips.

2. Preheat the oven to 350°F (Gas Mark 4).

3. Sauté the garlic in 5 tablespoons of the oil for 1 minute. Add the peppers and fry gently for a further 5 minutes. Correct seasoning.

4. Drop the pasta into rapidly boiling salted water.

5. Sauté the breadcrumbs in the remaining oil. Add the olives and capers and fry gently for about 4 minutes.

6. Drain the pasta when very *al dente.*

7. Spread half of the peppers over the bottom of a buttered oven dish. Add the spaghetti and cover with the remaining peppers. Top with the breadcrumb and olive mixture and bake in the oven for about 15 minutes, or until the top is golden brown. Allow to settle for 5 minutes before serving.

Puglia

Puglia is the region of Italy which produces the greatest quantity of durum wheat from which pasta is made. The following sauce is served with *orecchiette,* "little ears," a kind of homemade pasta made with semolina and water. This homemade pasta is quite difficult to make, and store-bought macaroni makes an excellent substitute. You might even be able to find *orecchiette* in an Italian shop.

Macaroni with broccoli
Maccheroni con i broccoli

For 4 persons
12 ounces (350 gr.) macaroni
1 pound (500 gr.) broccoli, with fairly large florets
4 anchovy fillets
3 tablespoons raisins (sultanas)
3 tablespoons pine nuts
2 tablespoons (30 gr.) butter
5 tablespoons olive oil
1 small onion, cut into thin rings
½ cup (50 gr.) Romano, or strong Cheddar cheese, freshly grated

1. Wash the broccoli and separate the florets from the stems and leaves. The stems and leaves can be cooked separately and used as a vegetable or in a salad. Drop the florets into a saucepan of rapidly boiling salted water. When the water returns to the boil, cook for a further 5 minutes. Drain thoroughly and set aside.

2. Soak the raisins in a cupful of warm water.

3. Sauté the onion rings in 4 tablespoons of the oil.

4. While the onion is cooking, heat the remaining oil in another small frying pan. Add the anchovy fillets, and reduce to a paste with a fork.

5. Drop the macaroni into rapidly boiling salted water. You may wish to use the water in which the broccoli was cooked.

6. Add the broccoli florets and anchovy paste to the onions, and stir gently over low heat. Drain the raisins and add these and the pine nuts to the broccoli sauce.

7. Drain the pasta, and turn into a warm serving bowl. Sprinkle with cheese and dot with butter. Mix well. Cover with the sauce and serve.

Spaghetti with tomatoes, anchovies and olives
Spaghetti alla pugliese

For 4 persons
12 ounces (350 gr.) spaghetti
1 pound (500 gr.) fresh tomatoes, peeled, or canned plum tomatoes
5 tablespoons olive oil
6 fillets of anchovy or 3 salted anchovies
1 tablespoon parsley, chopped
½ hot red chili pepper, crumbled
1 clove garlic, finely chopped
12 black olives, stoned
1 tablespoon capers
2 to 3 fresh basil leaves, torn into pieces
salt

1. If salted anchovies are used, bone them and rinse in cold water. Chop the fillets.

2. In a deep frying pan, fry the anchovies in the oil, mashing them with a fork. Add the tomatoes, garlic, basil and red pepper (use more or less according to taste) and cook, uncovered, for about 15 minutes, or until the sauce has thickened. Taste and adjust seasoning.

3. While the sauce is cooking, half cook the spaghetti.
Drain and transfer it to the frying pan. Cook the
spaghetti over high heat with the sauce until it is *al
dente,* stirring constantly.

4. Add the parsley, olives and capers. Mix well and
serve.

No cheese is needed.

Sicily

This sauce should be made only with young and very
fresh eggplant.

Vermicelli with eggplant (aubergines)
Vermicelli con le melanzane

For 4 persons
12 ounces (350 gr.) vermicelli
2 large eggplants (approximately 1 pound), peeled
2 cups vegetable oil for frying
5 tablespoons olive oil
1 clove garlic, finely chopped or crushed
2 tablespoons parsley, roughly chopped
1 hot red chili pepper, crumbled
salt

1. Cut the eggplant into very thin slices. Put them on a
slanting board and sprinkle with salt. Leave them to
drain for at least 1 hour, and pat dry with paper towels.
Deep fry them in the vegetable oil (in about 3 batches),
to which you have added the garlic and red pepper, for
about 5 minutes, or until golden, but not brown. Lift
them from the pan and lay them on paper towels.

2. Drop the pasta into rapidly boiling salted water.
Drain it (reserving some of the water), turn it into a hot
serving dish, and add 2 to 3 tablespoons of the water.
Toss with the olive oil, sprinkle with the parsley and
then lay the eggplant on the top. Serve at once.

In Sicily this dish is usually served without cheese,
but, if you wish, a bowl of grated Romano cheese can
be served on the side.

This sauce should be made with fresh tomatoes,
preferably plum.

Short pasta with fresh sardine sauce
Pasta corta con salsa di sarde

For 4 to 5 persons
12 ounces (350 gr.) short pasta (elbow or shell macaroni)
8 ounces (250 gr.) fresh sardines
5 or 6 basil leaves

3 tomatoes, peeled and chopped
1 onion, chopped
$\frac{3}{4}$ *cup olive oil*
salt and freshly ground black pepper

1. Bone, clean and wash the sardines, discarding the heads and tails.
2. In $\frac{1}{2}$ cup of the olive oil, sauté the onion, basil and tomatoes. Adjust seasoning.
3. Add the sardines, stir well, and simmer, covered, until the sauce becomes a smooth paste. If the sauce is too liquid, add 1 teaspoon of flour and cook for a further 5 minutes.
4. Cook and drain the pasta. Transfer it to a hot serving dish and toss with the remaining oil. Cover with the sauce, and serve at once. No cheese is needed.

Sardinia

Macaroni with *ragú* and mint

Maccheroncini alla moda di Nuoro

Mint is an herb not often found in Italian cooking. In Sardinia, where it grows wild everywhere, there are a few dishes in which it is used, and this is one of them.

For 4 persons
12 ounces (350 gr.) elbow or shell macaroni
8 ounces (250 gr.) chuck steak, cut into small cubes
1 pound (500 gr.) fresh peeled tomatoes or canned
    tomatoes, put through a food mill
5 tablespoons olive oil (or good vegetable oil)
1 clove garlic, crushed
1 tablespoon tomato paste
2 tablespoons red wine
2 tablespoons (30 gr.) butter
$\frac{1}{2}$ *cup (50 gr.) Romano cheese, freshly grated*
2 tablespoons fresh mint, chopped
salt and freshly ground black pepper

1. Fry the garlic in the oil for 1 minute. Add the meat and brown on all sides. Pour over the wine and reduce rapidly for 2 to 3 minutes. Add the tomatoes, tomato paste, and adjust seasoning. Simmer, uncovered, for approximately $\frac{3}{4}$ hour. (If the sauce becomes too dry add a little warm water.)

2. Cook the pasta in rapidly boiling salted water, drain it, and turn it into a warm dish. Toss with the butter, cover with the meat sauce and sprinkle with half of the cheese and with the mint. Mix thoroughly. Serve at once, with the rest of the cheese on the side.

Index

Recipe Index

Though born and brought up in Milan, Anna Del Conte is part Neapolitan — an important qualification for anyone writing a book on pasta. While studying at the University of Milan, she became particularly interested in the history of food, a subject which has remained her specialty ever since.

She combines academic knowledge about food with wide practical experience. This is built on the twin bases of a great love of cooking, and a fascination with traditional recipes, which she has been collecting and adapting to modern use for years.

She has lived in England for a considerable time now, and her experience in cooking for a large family there has taught her how to adapt the cooking of one country to the tastes — and ingredients — of another. Her many and varied pasta dishes have long been the envy of her friends, who finally persuaded her to write this book.